BAD HEMA

The historical masters' view of bad fencing and a modern interpretation for teachers and students

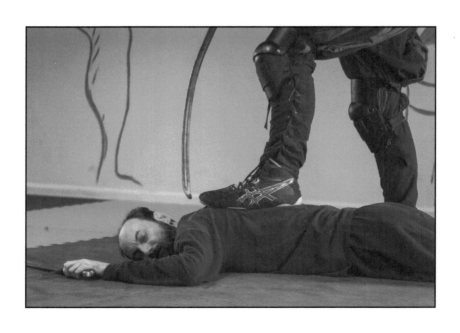

BAD HEMA

The historical masters' view of bad fencing and a
modern interpretation for teachers and students

by
Richard Marsden
Copyright 2021, All Rights Reserved

ISBN: 978-1-950626-13-7

Editor — Jeff Kemper
Formated by — Henry Snider
Cover Art by — Jay Simpson

Tyrant Industries

BAD HEMA

The historical masters' view of bad fencing and a modern interpretation for teachers and students

by

Richard Marsden

Table of Contents

"For the lovers of Historical European Martial Arts and the ancient art of the trash-talk."

Introduction

"You're all cowards and know little of this art."
—Fiore dei Liberi, Flower of Battle, 1410

"You have no idea what a real swordfight is like."
—Swrdmster72, Internet, 2008

The sentiments of Swrdmster72 were some of the first statements I came across when being introduced into HEMA (Historical European Martial Arts). In those days, communication was done largely through internet forums rather than the more diverse social media of today.

Great essays on the research of swordsmanship, the definition of terms, the interpretation of texts, and the best gear to be found were the norm. Rolling comments, some of them larger than the original post, was not unusual.

Many of the HEMA personalities and authors of today first appeared as nothing more than overly opinionated users on a handful of contentious forums. I should know, I was one of those overly opinionated users.

And through it all, we were a strange band of brothers and sisters, for in those days HEMA not only seemed much smaller, it *was* much smaller. There was no media awareness, there were few published books, and many of our beloved historical manuscripts were only seen through poor facsimiles or even crude hand-drawn copies. The HEMA clubs in North America were so few and far between that their founders all personally knew one another. If you had a strong opinion on HEMA, whether you lived in an RV on a swamp or in a high-rise New York apartment, the community as a whole knew about it.

And a common refrain amongst this unruly family was on how others were poor fencers. These fencers knew little of the art and were, in short, doing bad HEMA. It had to be called out!

Something always struck me about the comments of the would-be master lecturing on the supposed charlatans of the art—something familiar. That is because this practice of calling out the bad art in others is nothing new. It is HEMA to its core. Throughout the treatises, the masters did more than describe their swordsmanship techniques, they also singled out bad behavior. Often, this was done in a witty and humorous way, calling people fools and drunkards, or laughing about how they would utterly destroy their opponents because only they taught the ever elusive 'true art'. Often, this was done in a witty and humorous way, calling people fools and drunkards, or laughing about how they would utterly destroy their opponents because only they taught the ever elusive 'true art'.

I was struck by the bad HEMA because I was amused to notice the writers of today and of the past are often much closer than one might think, but also because I wondered if lessons could be learned from the bad behaviors mentioned by the masters of old.

Could bad HEMA lead to good? I think the answer is yes. Insults and wit aside, the masters who disparaged others did so because they wanted to exemplify their own art and felt compelled to show their readers just what sort of dangerous nonsense others were up to.

And well they should, for when learning HEMA we must remember that the masters did not always intend their students to fight others of equal skill. In fact, many sources cite the opposite—that the unskilled, dangerous, drunk, violent, timid, reckless, and misguided opponent was much more likely to be encountered than a fellow fencer skilled in the art.

Who are these poor fencers and what can we learn from them? After all, what not to do can be just as important as what to do.

And this was my guiding light, sickly flame that it is, in writing Bad HEMA. I wanted to share with the HEMA audience today, the complaints and admonishments of the historical masters. Some of these complaints are brief in nature; others require a bit of interpretation to work out. Some are explicit and clear on what makes constitutes bad fencing. Some contradict one another. For while di Grassi states many reasons that the thrust is superior to the cut, and how one who cuts all the time is bad at the art of fencing, Monesi states the opposite.

As is the case today, the masters of old are not in accord with one another on what makes bad fencing. Yet many were keenly aware of bad fencing and wanted to share with their readers to both warn and prepare them. Even when they disagree with one another we can still learn something.

Within these pages I hope the modern HEMA martial artist might learn something through the admonishments, complaints, and insults of the past masters. I bring you, *Bad HEMA*.

A Collection of Masters and Their Thoughts on Bad Fencing

I have included a variety of works from the 1400s to the 1700s to cover a wide array of masters. These masters sometimes spend little time discussing bad fencing, but others, like George Silver, spend a great deal, and Jacopo Monesi surpassed all of my expectations by writing exclusively about bad fencing.

The masters are not in agreement with one another on what constitutes bad fencing. Liechtenauer says those who wait in guard and deflect with the longsword are making a great mistake, while Fiore dei Liberi embraces such behavior. When the rapier was coming into fashion, a great debate arose on the value of the cut and thrust. Some masters, like di Grassi, thought the thrust was ideal, and others, like George Silver, thought the cut was just as important if not more so.

Still, there are elements of poor fencing that I believe all the masters would agree on as universally bad.

We must also remember that bad fencing may have been more common than we think. The masters who decried the poor behavior of others probably did so for a reason. The rapier master Giganti says as much:"[the fencer] has to contend with someone who does not know how to use the sword, which today you will find in the majority…"[1]

I heartily thank the translators of the HEMA and academic community as well as Wiktenauer for providing the public with a vast array of sources. From these sources I have tried to pluck the most explicit examples of bad fencing and provide my own commentary. Additionally, I've added a modern take on bad HEMA that addresses behaviors of those new to the art and how we at my club, the Phoenix Society of Historical Swordsmanship, try to improve them.

---

1   Nicoletto Giganti, The 'Lost' Second Book of Nicoletto Giganti (1608): A Rapier Fencing Treatise, Trans. Joshua Pendragon and Piermarco Terminiello (Leicestershire: Fox Spirit Books, 2013) 25.

JOHANNES LIECHTENAUER

Johannes Liechtenauer is traditionally regarded as the founder of the German style of fencing whose art included the longsword and other weapons. His methods, written down in a vaguely worded poem, formed the basis for German fencing from the late 1300s into the 1500s. His poem is called the *Zettel,* and by itself is hard to understand, but a series of follow-up masters provided explanations called glosses. By using the *Zettel* and the glosses together, an understanding of good, but also bad, fencing comes to light.

The *Zettel* is quick to point out bad fencers and false masters right at the beginning. The opening lines of the *zettel* explain why the poem is hard to understand.

"[H]e [Liechtenauer] has written of this art in hidden and secret words, so that not everyone will grasp and understand it, as you will find described below. And he has done this on account of frivolous fight masters who mistake the art as trivial, so that such masters will not make his art common or open with people who do not hold the art in respect as is its due."[2] Right away, the *Zettel* lets us know there were lesser men practicing the art and they had to be treated with suspicion and caution.

The first technical admonishment is on cutting. Liechtenauer believed a cut thrown out of time with the step would not be useful. For example, throwing a cut and then stepping would be the hallmark of a bad fencer: "He who follows the strokes should rejoice little in his art."[3]

A bad fencer is also one who does not understand where they are strong and weak. A left-handed fencer should not keep their blade high to the right, and a right-handed fencer should not keep their blade high and to the left. In either case the guard is weak, as are the strikes.

The poor fencer was timid, one who parries all the time and

---

2 Johannes Liechtenauer, Die Zettel [A Recital on the Chivalric Art of Fencing],Trans. Christian Tobler, 1448? In Wiktenauer: A HEMA Alliance Project, Accessed 2020, https://wiktenauer.com/wiki/Johannes_ Liechtenauer#Treatise.

3 Ibid.

does not attack. A sentiment shared by the *Zettel* and echoed by others was, "If you are easily intimidated, no fencing should you learn."[4]

This point is expanded upon when it comes to defense. A parry without a counter was dangerous in Liechtenauer's view: "I say to you truthfully, no one can defend himself without danger,"[5] and "Beware of parrying, if it happens to you, it troubles you greatly."[6]

If the parry fails or is deceived, then you will be struck. It was much better to be attacking and forcing the opponent to parry, or if attacked, performing a counter that both parried and struck the opponent at the same time. These are done with the hidden or master strokes. It is the bad fencer who waits in guard and seeks to parry or displace and the good fencer who uses the master strokes. They are the wrath (*Zornhau*), crooked (*Krumphau*), cross (*Zwerchhau*), squinting (*Schielhau*), and crown (*Schietelhau*) strikes.

Liechtenauer tells his students to adopt four guards, which he names, but to scorn the common guards. Alas, what these common guards are, he does not say. We know what they are not, namely, the German guards of the roof (*vom Tag*), the ox (*Ochs*), the plow (*Pflug*), and the fool (*Alber*). And by looking at the Italian, Fiore dei Liberi, we can see a contemporary who has many other guards, likely the kind Liechtenauer would consider common and to be avoided.

A poor fencer would press his blade too high in the bind and a good fencer would use that upward motion to strike him below: "Who to the War tends above, gets ashamed below."[7]

The wild fighter in the German sources is the buffalo. The buffalo comes on strong and may make quite a production, but he can also be defeated. A common refrain from the masters was that a strong and wild opponent may seem fearsome, but they usually opened themselves up to a skilled fencer by fighting without a sense of measure (distance) or tempo (timing). "And

---

4   *Ibid.*
5   *Ibid.*
6   *Ibid.*
7   *Ibid.*

the squinter breaks whatever a buffalo hits or stabs."[8]

Summary

Although brief, Liechtenauer describes bad, or common, fencing as something to be avoided. He thought it was unwise to parry alone. He believed it was much better to be aggressive, even on defense, and to always try to find openings of an opponent and in so doing fool the would-be masters. He also believed his art was a secret one that the common masters were unaware of, and thus their fencing was poor for they did not understand the true art.

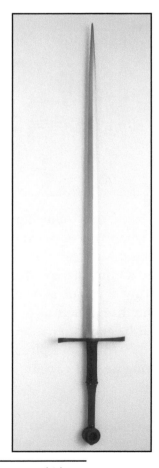

Albion's Munich Medieval Sword, a representation of the longsword depicted in many 14th – 16th century treatises.

Ibid

THE FELLOWSHIP OF LIECHTENAUER

Several masters are listed as students of Liechtenauer. This may mean they were actual students, or more likely, those inducted into the art of his secret teachings. These masters took up the *Zettel* and added explanations called glosses. Some of these glosses cite examples of bad fencing.

Peter Von Danzig, for example, says the following on the throwing of the spear: "Note that when you've positioned yourself and made ready to throw your spear, then cast the throw with concern. If you hit successfully, run in immediately. Do this even if you stand and do not want to throw. If you do not hit the opening correctly with the throw or the thrust, do not plunge with the spear, so you're not losing your balance so that he can throw you down, but take up the sword."[9] This act of plunging with the spear must have been something he had encountered before, otherwise why caution against it?

---

9   Peter Von Danzig, A gloss on Johannes Lichtenauer's Zettel, Trans. Christian Trosclair, In "Peter von Danzig zum Ingolstadt," Wiktenauer: A HEMA Alliance Project, Accessed 2020, https://wiktenauer.com/wiki/Peter_von_Danzig_zum_Ingolstadt.

He gives several other examples of staying balanced and advises being careful not to overextend, whether you are fighting with the sword or spear or you are wrestling.

In one example he states, "Do not commit to the strike so much that you come out of equilibrium, otherwise he will overcome you at the back and throw you down backwards or other such things as he has learned."[10] He gives numerous examples of what to do to an opponent who is unbalanced, either by your actions, or their own rash eagerness.

Sigmund Ringeck clarifies Liechtenauer's view of throwing a cut. He goes on to say that cut thrown without the foot passing, or passing too soon or too late, means the cut will miss and lack strength.

He is also very explicit in explaining why he believed it was a bad fencer who parries or tries to displace: "… you shall not focus nor wait upon his hew as he conducts it against you. Because all fencers who focus and wait upon another's hew and wish to do nothing else than displace, they permit such art little joy because they often become struck with it,"[11] and, "…with the *failer* (feint) all fencers who willingly displace become mislead and struck."[12] He advises keeping the sword on the correct shoulder, that being, if you are right-handed the sword is on your right shoulder, and if you are left-handed it is on your left; if you do the opposite you are weak, "because the art is quite awkward when a lefty conducts from the right side. It is also the same of a righty from the left side."[13]

And of the master or hidden strikes, Ringeck emphasizes their value, stating that most masters do not know them and so they fail at fencing: "Note, the Recital sets down five obscure hews. Many masters of the sword do know nothing to say about this…"[14]

---

10   Ibid.

11   *Sigmund Rigneck, A gloss on Johannes Lichtenauer's Die Zettel, Translated by Christian Trosclair, In "Sigmund Rigneck," Wiktenauer: A HEMA Alliance Project, https://wiktenauer.com/wiki/Sigmund_ain_Ringeck#Long_ Sword_Gloss.*

12   Ibid.

13   Ibid.

14   Ibid.

Summary

The Fellowship do not bring up new examples of bad fencing so much as clarify the purposefully obscure examples in the Zettel. The warnings are the same though as they were with Liechtenauer. The bad fencer is one who cuts without properly stepping. He chases the sword with parries and deflections. He fences on the wrong side. And finally, he does not know the hidden strikes, which is why he chases swords.

FIORE DEI LIBERI

Fiore dei Liberi was the son of an Imperial Knight and was active in northern Italy. He became a fencing master for the Italian elite and his students included famous condottiere (mercenary lords). He decided in his elder years to put a treatise together, the *Flower of Battle*, which was produced in 1410. Four copies survive and each is a little different from the other but contain many of the same guards, plays (techniques), counters, and imagery.

Of bad fencing, Fiore echoes Liechtenauer on the temperament of a fencer, stating they should not be fearful or afraid, nor should the art be taught to peasants. He was an elite teacher who wanted his art kept a secret, so much so that he fought five unarmored duels against jealous masters who wanted to know his techniques. Fiore came away unscathed and the victor of all five duels, keeping both his honor and his secrets.

Throughout the *Flower of Battle*, he insults bad fencers, noting they know little of the art. In one case, he challenges a hundred of these bad fencers to attack him one at a time, and each one he would defeat from one guard. "You're all cowards and know little of this art. You're all just words without any deeds. I challenge you to come at me one after another, if you dare, and even if there are a hundred of you, I'll destroy all of you from this powerful guard."[15]

Here and there, Fiore shows a technique in which he calls out the opponent as a fool, or someone who will very shortly regret their decisions in life. These fencers did not know enough of the art, which Fiore saw as a great body of knowledge of which people knew only a little. Though he does not call himself a perfect master of the art, he says others call him such. He goes on to say that if there were doctorate degrees awarded for the understanding of fencing, he would have one. Which perhaps explains why his opponents are chided for not knowing enough and Fiore lets them know he could humiliate them. In one case, he even threatens to use an opponent as a writing desk. "I have locked you in the lower bind, or strong key, and from this position you can't escape regardless of how strong you are. I could hurt you or even kill you. I could stop to write a letter and you wouldn't even be able to see what I was doing. You've lost your sword and your helmet, you've been humiliated, and you'll soon be hurting."[16]

Fiore even shows techniques he considers unusual or perhaps not safe, but to be a complete master he wanted to share them. This also gives us a hint of what a bad fighter might attempt. "This is a play that involves a throw over the leg, which is not a very safe move in grappling …"[17]

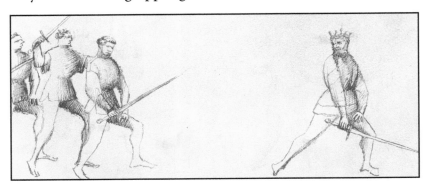

15   Fiore dei Liberi, *The Flower of Battle: MS Ludwig XV13*, Trans. Colin Hatcher (Phoenix: Tyrant Industries, 2017), 20.

16   *Ibid. 33.*

17   *Ibid. 7.*

Several fencers depicted in the *Flower of Battle* are making a mistake, and therefore they are being struck.

A fencer who strikes low, is deceiving themselves because the opponent can pull their leg back and cut at the head. This concept of "don't go low if they go high" is seen in numerous martial arts of the period and is one of Fiore's warnings on what not to do. The lesson is that the bad fencer aims below the knee and is hit in the head for his trouble. "With a two-handed sword it's unwise to strike to the knee or below, because it is too dangerous for the one striking."[18]

A fencer who comes on with a heavy over-handed strike, the peasant's blow, engages in self-deception, for the good fencer can defeat the bad, in this case, by stepping off to the side and using the sword as a hanging parry to let the peasant's blow slide away. The lesson is clear—the bad fencer hits overly hard and slowly.

More can be gleaned by looking at the positions the opponents take in the Flower of Battle. Many of these are not any of Fiore's named guards, so we can assume they are examples of bad fencing.

And the weakness of the guard is shown in a play. Here an opponent's guard has allowed an opening for the master to strike at him. And with the spear he shows the opponents in guards he does not name, and so again we can assume they are examples of bad fencing.

Summary

Fiore's entire art is one meant to fight not itself, but to fight a sea of fools who know little or not enough of the art. Where he calls out bad behavior, it is sometimes because their technique is bad, but often it is because they do not know the art and so can be deceived by it. As often is the case, Fiore waits in a guard, then counters the opponent's actions who very rarely know what to do next, much less what counter they might perform. Time and again the master takes their attacks and defeats them.

---

18   Ibid. 26.

His art is contrary to the German tradition which explicitly says waiting in a guard to deflect is bad fencing, while Fiore literally challenges a hundred opponents to come at him one by one and be defeated by his guard and deflections.

The two methods have the same goal, but with different means of getting there. The German tradition seeks to interrupt and take away a bad fencer's initiative, while Fiore seeks to invite an attacker in, and so deceive them with a well-planned response to their expected strike.

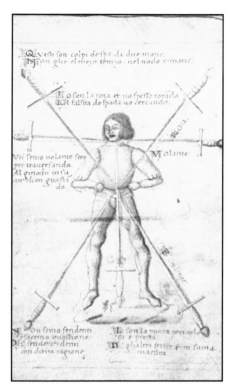

PHILLIPO VADI

Phillipo Vadi produced his treatise, *On the Art of Swordsmanship*, between 1482 and 1487, and it was a gift to an Italian lord, the Duke of Urbino. Vadi's work takes much from Fiore, sometimes verbatim, but does not mention him by name. Furthermore, Vadi is not parroting Fiore, but rather, expanding upon or in some cases altering or even redacting elements of the *Flower of Battle*. Furthermore, he breaks from Fiore's view that fencing is an art and says it is in fact a science, governed by immutable principles.

Like Fiore and Liechtenauer, he tells us to not be a fearful fencer, but he also calls out the qualities of a bad one: "…whoever is thick-brained, pusillanimous, and cowardly must be banished from such nobility and refinement of the art."[19] And yes, he later goes on to clarify when he says "art" he actually means "science."

There are oblique references to poor fencers (or fighters in general) as the case may be. He says, "As the famous saying goes, cleverness overcomes strength . . . Oftentimes in these texts, a small person of little strength overcomes, prostrates, and throws a big, tough, and brave man to the ground."[20]

The theme of the clever overpowering the strong shows up repeatedly throughout his text. A small man must be clever, if a big man attacks, the smaller man must use cunning, and so

19   Guy Windsor, Veni Vidi Vici, (The School of European Swordsmanship, 2013),, 26.
20   Ibid. 29.

on. To Vadi, someone relying on their strength alone was a bad fencer because they could be overcome through a devious technique. One might even think Vadi was a small man himself, when for the third time he restates, "A man's great strength can break the guards, but natural cleverness will keep that in check, it gives good boldness to a small man."[21]

Bad fencers, in his view, had bad traits. He gives an example where a man might know his art well but warns there is always one who knows it better. Thus, it was bad behavior, and thus bad fencing, to needlessly pick a fight: "He who wishes to use the art to oppose everyone, out of a thousand one will best him, and so he loses his honor for one single mistake. He who is below may believe to be above, and this is the kind who is often combative with others, often he will start a disagreement with another, and what started as such becomes a quarrel, here is where he who knows the art will show his mettle."[22]

And he further elaborates, "He who wishes to offend others without reason, certainly damns his soul and body, and brings shame upon his master."[23]

For bad fencing techniques, he calls out the style of the past to be wrong. When using the longsword it was traditional to stand with the opposite foot forward than the hand controlling the sword. So, a right handed fencer holding the longsword would place it on their right shoulder, but their left foot would be leading. This was so that when they struck, they could do so with a pass and end up right foot forward upon striking. Vadi suggests it was better to keep the right foot forward because it was closer and faster. This striking without a proper passing step goes against the advice of prior masters such as Liechtenauer and his Fellowship.

Why the difference? Vadi is coming upon the concept that the pass, when the rear foot becomes the lead, has power, but takes time, and that the advance, when the lead foot moves ahead and the rear follows, was faster. Unlike Liechtenauer, Vadi believed the advance of the foot was sufficient when throwing a cut.

---

21   Ibid. 56.
22   Ibid. 50.
23   Ibid. 50.

Vadi says all of his teachings will come to nothing without practice, "One who does not practice [the art] will get into trouble."[24] The same admonishment is given by the likes of many other masters in this book. The bad fencer is one who does not practice. Like Fiore, when he depicts a play, he sometimes calls out the bad fencing that led to it.

"You believed I would strike with a *roverso* (left to right) blow, [But] With my elbow I push your sword across."[25]

Summary

Vadi is similar to Fiore in displaying bad fencing failing when confronting his art. He breaks with what he saw as two traditions. First, Vadi believed fencing was a science and not an art. Second, he did not believe it was necessary to keep the sword on the shoulder and the opposite foot leading. It might not be exactly fair to say Vadi saw the fencing of his ancestors as bad, but rather that thanks to advances in understanding measure and tempo, the art was becoming a science with better ways.

24   Ibid. 97.
25   Ibid. 137.

PIETRO MONTE

Pietro Monte was not a fencing master at all. He was a captain of men. He was a writer and soldier and known to the likes of Baldassare Castiglione, author of the famed *Book of the Courtier*, and Leonardo da Vinci, who wanted to discuss with Monte some weapon designs.

We are not sure where he was from, but it appears he had a strong connection to Spain while his career was in Italy. He lived and died by the sword, perishing in one of the many petty wars in Italy.

As a soldier and not a fencing master, he has a unique view on martial arts. His techniques are simple, and he even calls out fencing masters of having bad habits.

"Absolutely no guard or defensive stance is safe in armed combat, for if we try to close ourselves up we guarantee our own defeat. It often happens that master fighters or those who follow the profession of teaching others in arms commit the error of getting hit by placing themselves in a closed guard."[26]

Monte suggests simple guards in which the sword is kept in opposition to the opponent. A century later, the rapier master

---

26   *Pietro Monte, Collectanea: The Arms, Armour and Fighting Techniques of a Fifteenth-Century Soldier, Trans. Jeffery L. Forgeng (Woodbridge: The Boydell Press, 2018), p 131.*

Giganti had similar advice, dispensing with the named guards and instead suggesting that a counter-guard be adopted. In practice, this means if the opponent's sword is held high, then you would do the same, if their sword was pointed at your chest, then your sword would be pointed at theirs and your blade would always be in opposition of the opponent's.

Monte derides fanciful techniques. When describing the use of the pole-axe, his advice is simple, and he suggests the weapon be used to beat aside attacks and respond with a thrust- very much like a spear. French and German pole-axe techniques use a lot more rotational strikes, jabs, and hooks with the axe. Monte has no use for these.

The French in particular, as well as many Germans, play with the pole-axe... as if they were in a mere fist-fight. In truth, children, women and peasants do the same thing when one of them holds some staff or weapon... and so they go wheeling their arms around, now high, now low. An experienced fighter never gets into such a contest of revolving the arms.[27]

He is also not a fan of heavy armor, which he calls white armor. He says that white armor, especially for the chest and head, was only for the initial rush of lances or as proof against guns and crossbow bolts. Lighter armor was much preferable because it allows a fighter to move in and out of combat while at the same time, they can maneuver their body so their armor can be presented as needed. Those armored head to foot in plate he found almost comical saying that they strike one another like blacksmiths pounding away on an anvil. Such is noisy more than effective.

While primarily a book on raising and training soldiers, Monte's work does delve into dueling. Here, he says fighting on horseback is a bad idea because you then must worry about yourself and the horse. If you do fight a duel on horseback, he strongly suggests that rules be in place in which the horse cannot be targeted.

---

27   *Ibid. 112.*

Summary

Monte's writings are not focused on dueling, and he is clear in that he thinks little of fencing masters and teachers. His techniques and guards are simple, and he compares them to the complex, wheeling and ineffectual guards of contemporary fencing masters.

Much of his advice is simple but he is thorough, covering everything from Galen's four humors, to fighting techniques with all manner of weapons, to what qualities a commander should have and what types of armor exist and where the best metal can be found (Innsbruck by his reckoning).

Joachim Meyer

Joachim Meyer's *fechtbuch* (fencing book) is the *Thorough Description of the Art of Fencing*, published in 1570. It was his second and most complete work, covering the use of the dussack, longsword, rapier, and dagger, as well as various pole arms.

When it comes to bad fencing, he considered the fencing of foreigners (likely Italians) to be poor. It was not because their techniques were bad, but rather that they were immoral, since the use of the thrust was fatal and Germans tried to keep their duels limited to the cut. The tradition was the same in Poland where among themselves, the Poles delivered various cuts with their sabers, but  reserved the thrust for times of war against foreigners. According to George Silver, before the Italians arrived England was much the same.

Meyer says, "For although the thrust was permitted by our forefathers in earnest cases against the common enemy, yet not only did they not permit it in sporting practice, but they would also in no way allow it for their sworn-in soldiers or others who had come in conflict with each other, except against the common enemy…"[28]

Meyer was also upset with the gun, which while not exactly "bad fencing," did cruelly nullify good fencing. He writes that "in

---

28   *Joachim Meyer, The Art of Combat: A German Martial Arts Treatise of 1570, Trans. Jeffery L. Forgeng (Barnsley, UK: Frontline Books, 2015), 137.*

recent times the ignoble gun has arisen and so taken the upper hand, that by its agency the most manly and skilled hero can be suddenly deprived and robbed of his life sometimes even by the pettiest and timid of men."[29]

Meyer repeatedly mentions that his book should correct many of the bad fencing habits people had taken up during his day, and that had his book been printed in the past, it may have rectified the problem early on. In short, people fence poorly and my book could have prevented it!

And why were people so bad at fencing? Meyer says it was because dishonorable people had taken up disorderly lives. They were gambling, whoring, cursing, uttering blasphemy, displaying lewdness, and they had thrown themselves into peasant brawling rather than the true art of combat.

This sentiment was shared by another German, Paulus Hector Mair, in his, *Opus of Athletic Arts*, a book he embezzled governmental coffers to produce and would later be hanged for. He said the Germans were losing their skill at fencing because they had given themselves over to drinking, gambling, the lust for women, and the desire for the latest fashion. He went on to complain about how a pair of Roman fencing masters participated in a murderous riot causing much destruction and gave fencing a bad name, and that the profession of being a fencing master was in peril.

For both Mair and Meyer, bad fencing was as much a character fault as it was the use of poor techniques. They are not alone in this opinion, and numerous masters warn about fencers with character faults such as disagreeableness.

To learn the true art of fencing, knowledge and practice must go hand in hand. Meyer states that no technique, no matter how good it is, will work if it is used at the wrong time, a point he belabors more than once. A fencer had to know the four openings (high left and right, low left and right) to attack an opponent. Knowing where was only part of the art, because more importantly, a fencer had to know *when* to attack the four openings.

---

29   *Ibid.* 37.

Meyer described four general type of fencers. None of them are necessarily bad fencers, but they could be if they didn't understand proper fencing, which to him revolved around proper timing. Of the four types of fencers, the first fencer is one who as soon as they can, thrusts and cuts. This fencer might be striking at the wrong time and opening themselves up to counters and devices. Such fencers are stupid, overzealous, and violent.

The second fencer is one who waits for his opponent to make a mistake and follows up with a counter or device. This is a judicious fencer in Meyer's view.

The third fencer is one who strikes at openings when the time is right, and in such a way that they can recover. This was Meyer's particular favorite, though he notes he may adopt other attitudes depending on his opponent. This is a judicious and deceitful fencer.

And finally, the fourth fencer is a fool who waits in guard, for they are either a foolish fencer who will be hit at the onset, or they are in truth a master, waiting to use a clever counter.

All of these could be the traits of a good or bad fencer, and Meyer says you must adopt the right persona for the right time and place. While the first fencer might be described as stupid, against a very timid opponent, he may be the right guy at the right time! Just as the waiting fool might in fact be a clever master.

When it comes to footwork, Meyer agrees with Liechtenauer, "Whoever first steps after the cuts should not rejoice much of his skill."[30] This means that a poor fencer is stationary when they cut, or they cut and then try and step, but in both cases they rob themselves of proper power. Meyer says a fencer who steps too late or too soon ruins their own device (technique).

When describing his techniques and devices, Meyer does not belabor bad fencing. In fact, the opponent is likely a skilled fencer and Meyer's techniques are meant to fight someone who knows what they are doing but they lack perfect knowledge and so make mistakes. He says, for example that "if your opponent

---

30   *Ibid.* 68.

cuts with his weapon either far too up or down, or too far out to the side, then you rush after him at his opening and thus prevent his cut coming to completion."[31] Commentary on those making mistakes can be found throughout his discourse. On feints, Meyer says anyone can perform what he calls a *fehlen* stroke, but that only those good at the art can pull them off convincingly. A poor fencer tries to feint cuts too slowly or he cuts at the sword rather than at the opponent. In either case, he does not get the proper reaction if he is facing a skilled fencer. Other masters agree with this idea that a proper feint thrown correctly was masterful, but more often than not it was done poorly.

Similarly, someone who wishes to perform a changing, or *wechseln* needs to be experienced. This is when an enemy's attack is avoided because they are cutting at the sword rather than the body. Done poorly, the fencer takes too much time going from one line of attack to another and is consequently hit. To be used correctly the *wechseln* is used when the opponent is fencing poorly and seeking your sword rather than you. "If he cuts at your sword and not at your body, then in his cut let your point slip through underneath with crossed hands; step and cut long into the other opening."[32]

Being overly aggressive is also a sign of a bad fencer. Cutting at the four openings described by Meyer, but without any thought, was not good fencing. Such an opponent could be overcome by pressing close to them and parrying their sword, then pressing in and pushing the opponent away to create a proper opening for a cut. Aggressive fencers might make a good show but lacked the proper timing to make much of their work. A theme carried by multiple masters.

The fencer unaware of when to strike and when not to, when to parry and when to press or retreat will learn nothing. Meyer strongly believed the techniques had their proper time and place, those being, before (*Vor*), after (*Nach*), simultaneous (*Gleich*), and during (*Indes*) and that the poor fencer was unable to tell the four moments apart. The *Indes* was of greatest importance

---

31   *Ibid.* 62.
32   *Ibid.* 66.

because it was a moment when time could be stolen back from the opponent—when the *Nach* could become the *Vor*. Those unable to sense that time could not be good fencers. "And if you do not heed it (*Indes*) and execute all cuts wisely and judiciously, you will easily run into your own harm, as can be seen in those combatants who are overly aggressive and as the saying goes, will extend up but never on (reach but never hit)."[33]

On the subject of counters, Meyer believed they were of only partial value. To Meyer, it was too hard to tell exactly what kind of attack the opponent might use, and so it was better to know a few counters but many techniques, and that if the *Indes* could be understood, along with all the other times he mentions, poor fencing could be avoided. For those who liked to linger in a guard in hopes of a counter, Meyer suggested such poor fencers could be defeated by throwing a feint to bait the counter and then to cut at an opening.

Summary

Meyer's overall advice on fencing is described in a proverb, "...to have begun well may in all things practically half-acquit you, yet equally on the other hand a poor finish may ruin and bring nothing..."[34] In other words, knowing a technique is not enough, for just because you can perform it, does not mean you can successfully use it. Meyer believed only through diligent practice could a fencer learn to properly perform and successfully land their techniques and devices.

Throughout his treatise, the "bad fencer" was one who didn't understand timing, neither before (Vor), after (Nach), simultaneous (Gleich) or instantly (Indes). These fencers, because they mistimed everything, either never landed their cuts and thrusts, or performed them in a way that they

---

33   Ibid. 68.
34   Ibid. 68.

could easily be interrupted.

In an example, Meyer notes the aggressive fencer, likely the buffalo mentioned in earlier German sources, might have the Vor, but if they don't know how to use the rest of the timing in the fight, they will have the Vor snatched from them in the Indes by an opponent who does. How? Imagine an opponent who strikes powerfully and aggressively but out of measure. As they miss, they can then be struck. The Vor is thus seized in the Nach.

GIACOMO DI GRASSI

Giacomo di Grassi was an Italian fencing master who moved to England and wrote treatises that were published in both Italian and English. Di Grassi was writing in the late 1500s when the rapier was fast gaining popularity throughout Europe. The rapier of his day might be called a side-sword today and was a little shorter and a little stouter than the rapiers seen throughout the 17th century. Much of his writing is advancing the argument that the thrust is superior to the cut; such is the case in his *True Art of Defense*, published in Italy in 1570 and in England in 1594.

When writing, he described behaviors he thought should be avoided. First and foremost of these behaviors was cutting when one should thrust. Di Grassi reasons that if a man were to throw a powerful blow he would be stabbed by an opponent. Why? A moment in time is called a tempo. To throw a blow, the sword must be raised then launched in an attack, which takes two tempo. A thrust takes only one. Thus, the thrust will strike as the cutter raises his sword. This basic concept was the foundation for other rapier treatises. That isn't to say that cuts should never be performed. Di Grassi even gives examples of when it is appropriate to do so, but he is also clear in noting that a fencer who always cuts will find himself stabbed. This even applies to cutting weapons when used in a one-on-one scenario. The great sword, for example, is a weapon meant to be used in powerful, sweeping strikes to cut aside pikes, but di Grassi says when a great swordsman fences a solitary great swordsman, he's better off throwing a one-handed and very deceptive thrust.

When a cut is to be performed di Grassi says those who throw cuts with the shoulder are making a mistake, because, while such blows are powerful, they take too much time and you could be attacked with a thrust or a faster cut thrown from the elbow or wrist.

Cuts from left to right he calls *riverso*. Of these cuts, he says only a fool would use them alone because they not only take time, but they also leave the body open to be struck by an opponent's thrust or counter-cut.

When using the sword and buckler, a bad fencer will not realize the danger of the thrust. They will throw cut after cut, and then end up walking onto a thrust when their opponent takes an oblique step, while parrying with the buckler and thrusting with the sword at the same time.

The targa is a larger buckler, square in shape with angles. Di Grassi says some prop the targa on their thigh, some hold it close to their chest and neck, and both are wrong. He further notes that "my opinion will show how much they fooled themselves."[35] He goes on to say the targa should be held extended and angled slightly to cover both the head and body.

Of the shield, he says some use it improperly like the targa, resting it on their thigh. Others keep the shield close to the body, but also blind themselves to their enemy, as if hiding behind a wall. His advice is similar to that of the targa, to keep the shield extended and angled, so it covers the head and body, but does not block your vision.

When it comes to movement, di Grassi particularly calls out those who tried to make themselves large and small by contorting their bodies. "Accordingly, I don't think highly of the manner of fencing used by those who are constantly making themselves small sometimes and then big at others, turning now one way and now another, looking as if they were snakes."[36] He goes on to say that such behavior takes time, and in the time it takes to shrink back, or straighten up, you could be attacked.

As for training, di Grassi lets his readers know, "I do not in any way recommend the opinion held by those who would have someone who wishes to make his arm strong handle a heavy sword at the outset, because once so accustomed, ordinary ones seem light."[37] And he suggests the opposite, to use a lighter weapon to train speed over raw power. This advice is counter to that of Manciolino, who in 1531 in his treatise suggests the

35   Giacomo di Grassi, True Art of Defense, Trans. Norman White. Wiktenauer: A HEMA Alliance Project. Accessed 2020. https://wiktenauer. com/wiki/Giacomo_di_Grassi#The_True_Art_of_Defense..
36   Ibid.
37   Ibid.

use of a heavy sword so that a real one might feel lighter. Not all Italians were in agreement on what constituted good and bad practices!

Summary

The reoccurring theme of what is "bad fencing" is taking too much time to act. Di Grassi clearly understood the concept of tempo and how a single-tempo action was superior to a multi-tempo action because the former was faster. He tries to explain this through imagery and geometric lines to try and mathematically prove the value of the thrust over the cut.

He also understood the danger of waiting too long and preferred an offensive tempo to a non-offensive one. If you are within measure and try to change guard, make yourself smaller, or rear your arm back to cut, then your opponent could commit to a single tempo thrust and hit you. Di Grassi was aware of this and calls out bad fencing for its poor use of tempo and the wasting of time.

GEORGE SILVER

George Silver was an English fencing master who was faced with a peculiar problem. The English method of fighting with the sword and buckler was being supplanted by Italian ways and even masters. These Italians, such as di Grassi, were teaching the use of the rapier and using an academic methodology and schools to show how their methods were superior. Silver saw this influx of foreigners as bad for England, both morally, for their style of fencing encouraged dueling, and practically, for their style of fencing would get you killed. He penned his complaints in *Paradoxes of Defense*, published in 1599, which followed up an earlier treatise on his own methods of fighting, the *Brief Instructions Upon my Paradoxes of Defense*.

To Silver, the foreign fencers were all bad, and the proof was in the pudding. If their methods worked, then why was Rome sacked and why did Henry V beat the French at Agincourt? Furthermore, the rapier itself was not a tool of war and had no place on the battlefield; as a civilian weapon, he believed they were toys that could be defeated by a shorter, stouter, and thoroughly English sword.

He warns would-be fencers to avoid the Italian masters invading England:

[T]he Italian Teachers of Offense done unto them, and great errors, inconveniences, and false resolutions they have brought them into, has informed me, even for pity of their most lamentable wounds and slaughters, and as I verily think it my bound duty, with all love and humility to admonish them to take heed, how they submit themselves into the hand of Italian teachers of defense, or strangers whatsoever, and to beware how they forsake or suspect their own natural fight, that they may by casting off these Italianated, weak, fantastical, and most devilish and imperfect fights . . .[38]

And to be quite clear, he really disliked them. "They (the

---

38   George Silver, *Paradoxes of Defense* (London: Printed for Edward Blount 1599), Accessed 2020, http://www.pbm.com/~lindahl/paradoxes. html.

Italians) are imperfect in their profession, their fight is false, and they are false teachers, deceivers and murderers, and to be punished accordingly."[39]

The bad fencing of these foreigners on English soil came from the rapier itself as much as from those who used them. He cites four reasons for this. First, the Italian masters went about in their home country wearing armor, a sign that their methods were not good. Second, when they did fight, they often killed one another. Third, they did not give a measurement of how long a sword should be, and so Silver said a perfect fight could not be had since a man might get a sword that was too long or short. Finally, the cross-guard of the rapiers was inadequate to withstand heavy blows. Overall, he said their swords were too long and too heavy, and so once entangled became useless.

Silver says a rapier has no sure defense in and of itself. Two masters might line up to face one another and if they both attacked, they would both be dead. The belief that the rapier could defend while it attacks was something Silver said was false and gave an anecdote of: "Two captains at Southampton even as they were going to take shipping upon the key, fell at strife, drew their rapiers, and presently, being desperate, hardy or resolute, as they call it, with all force and over great speed, ran with their rapiers one at the other, and were both slain."[40] This event was not unique, and Silver says it is from the bad habit of the rapier masters to attack if the enemy point was not in line. However, Silver says a simple turn of the wrist brings the point back on line and the attacker impales himself, and perhaps his opponent as well.

The Spanish method of fencing he says appears good, for the Spaniard stands erect with his rapier far extended and pointed at the enemy. And if the opponent tries to walk into this guard, they will indeed be struck. However, Silver says the rigid posture can easily be disrupted, and that once the point of the rapier is not in line, all the Spanish tricks fail to work outside an academic setting. He likens it to a joke about a woman who told a doctor who was sea-sick to put a stone in his mouth. So

---

39   *Ibid.*
40   *Ibid.*

long as the stone stayed in his mouth, he would not be sick. The doctor tried it, but upon getting sea-sick, threw up, stone and all. Indeed, so long as the stone was in his mouth, he was not sick.

While giving more explicit reasons why the Italians were in fact poor fencers, he cites a few reasons. The Italian masters did not understand true and false times. They did not understand the governors of combat. They did not understand the distance of a fight. In short- they knew nothing at all except how to kill and get themselves killed.

In Silver's own words, the true and false fight could be differentiated:

> *The true fights be these: whatsoever is done with the hand before the foot or feet is true fight. The false fights are these: whatsoever is done with the foot or feet before the hand, is false, because the hand is swifter than the foot, the foot or feet being the slower mover than the hand, the hand in that manner of fight is tied to the time of the foot or feet, and being tied thereto, has lost his freedom, and is made thereby as slow in his motions as the foot or feet, and therefor that fight is false.*[41]

To Silver, the first governor of the fight is being able to look an opponent over and see if his guard was good or bad and understand what he can and cannot do. The second is understanding the measure of fight and how close you have to be to offend, but also how close the opponent has to be to offend you. Third and fourth, he combines to say that you need to be able to press the attack on your opponent but also retreat when needed to be safe.

Above all, a safe fight was more important than anything. Something Silver says the bad Italian fencers did not practice. So eager for combat, they would run themselves through in a quarrel, while two good English fencers, each seeing the other was unassailable, would go home for the night. He goes on to

---

41   *Ibid.*

say the Italian method of fencing encouraged violence, so that not only were the Italian masters false, their weapon was false and they brought about discord amongst friends! Imagine fencing so bad it brought about the downfall of civilization!

The cut and thrust was another matter that irked Silver. He believed the cut and thrust were both important, but the cut more so. This was in contradiction to the likes of di Grassi who favored the thrust. Silver goes so far as to have a fictitious conversation between an Englishman and Italian, wherein the Englishman states that cuts can lop off a hand and arm and take just as much time to throw as a thrust, while the Italian thrust may run a man through many times over, only for said man to cut the Italian down and go home for the eve.

Silver noted what he called an "evil practice" in the fencing schools of his day. The English ones were forbidding the thrust, and the Italian ones the cut. While he understood the debate between the thrust and cut, Silver thought neither should be disallowed, because both have their uses. He is not alone in this, and Italian masters, who he claimed believed in the thrust alone, often noted that the cut did have its value whereas the thrust was superior. However, hyperbole of an argument was as common in the past as it is today.

Silver said Italians and their blinded English students were without skill and even when they did happen to get close to another in the semblance of a proper fight, it was quite by accident.

> *Two unskillful men many times by chance strike or thrust together, chance unto them, because they know not what they do, or how it comes to pass. But the reasons or causes are these. Sometimes two false times meet and make a just time together, and sometimes a true time and a false time meet and make a just time together, and sometimes two true times meet and make a just time together. And all this happens because the true time and place is unknown unto them.*[42]

---

42   *Ibid.*

And why did this clearly false method of fighting sweep England's gentry like a mania? Silver believed it was because the Italian teachers were able to deceive their students by making their art appear true. They did this through demonstrations that were done slowly and in such a way as to show how in theory their art worked, but in practice Silver assures us they would fail and that even an unskilled fencer was better than one "trained" in the Italian method. The Italian fight was using the false time.

Lastly, and in contradiction to nearly every other master, Silver calls out specific individuals and their false teachings as well as ways in which they were embarrassed by England's native fencers. While other masters do decry false-masters, they rarely name them and when they do, they are cautious, as Alfieri says of Achille Marozzo when complaining about him, "but I shall not speak ill of the dead."[43] Silver was different and indeed gleeful in airing the names and misadventures of the false-masters.

Summary

Silver's work is one that is specifically about bad fencing. He lays out his argument that the Italian reliance on the thrust, their swords, their movements and lack of understanding led to a system that was not only bad, but dangerous to all. To Silver, the Italian masters were entirely off on their sense of measure (both of the person and the sword) and the timing of the fight. He believed they worked using false time, trying to use their foot or body to defeat the motion of the hand, which in Silver's view was too fast for the foot or body to counter. The Italians knew how to attack but not defend, and so they often killed themselves in a duel.

Was there any nativist reason behind all this? Yes, because these Italian masters were taking away students who would otherwise have gone to an English school of defense. That said, all

---

43   Francesco Ferdinando Alfieri, La Scherma: The Art of Fencing, Trans. and ed. Caroline Stewart, Phil Marshall, and Piermarco Terminiello (San Bernardino: Vulpes, 2017), 101.

masters have their biases but that doesn't mean
they are necessarily wrong, and Silver backs up his
assertations with explicit examples (names and
all!) as well as his theory on what was good fencing
and what was bad.

MARCO DOCCIOLINI

Docciolini's *Treatise on the Subject of Fencing* was written in 1601 and comprised the Florentine's experiences in fencing from the 1500s. His method was one of the earlier rapier treatises, in which the rapier and side sword were not as distinct as they appear to be in later years. His work is mostly about what "to do" but does include examples of what not to do, or what would be bad fencing.

For example, when describing guards he notes two straight guards, one low and one high. In each the body is light and agile, held in profile to the opponent with the right foot leading, and the sword is held far extended, in line with the foot or elevated with the shoulder. Of these guards, Docciolini says he will not make much of them because they are only good for defense, and a good guard is one that can offend and defend.

In a more clear case of bad fencing, he says some fencers stand in guard with their sword withdrawn to the thigh, a practice he goes on to refute saying that "my sword will not be found." This is in error though because as Docciolini says, "…the sword must travel much further than if it were held in front of them."[44]

Another guard he cautions against is holding the sword high, but wide. He says some do this to look more fearsome, but in fact it is poor fencing. The fencer who holds their sword out wide and high has farther to go when defending themselves against an attack than if they had kept their sword pointed at the enemy and their hand more in line with the body.

When attacking he says, "Take care not to act as some do, by delivering the *imbroccata* (High thrust) all the way to the ground, stating that this way it has greater reach. In saying this they fool themselves, because as the *imbroccata* passes below chest height, you begin to reduce its extension. The more you lower it, the more dangerous it becomes."[45]

---

44   Marco Docciolini, *Treatise on the Subject of Fencing: Marco Docciolini's 1601 Fencing Treatise*, Trans. Piermarco Terminiello and Steven Reich (San Bernardino: Vulpes, 2017) 32.

45   Ibid. 38.

The thrust should not be powered by the hand alone, because this flinging lacks power and so better to thrust by turning the body and extending the whole arm.

Docciolini says when fencing, the blade should be pointed at the right shoulder of the opponent, what he calls the *punto*. It is there where attacks should be directed.

But what about targeting the hand?

"I say no, because the hand does not stay still, as it is raised and lowered. As such, you cannot keep your point steady."

Those who move their sword from one side of the opponent's blade to the other, or the inside and outside, is performing what he calls a *sfalasta*. This method is one Doccioloni calls out as used by unskilled fencers who are unsure what to do, and so hope to disorder their opponent. Against a skilled opponent he says this will not work and gives several techniques to stop it, namely, turning your wrist so the true edge of your blade faces your opponent, and then thrusting. This can be done quickly, since the turn of wrist is fast, while the poor fencer wastes time moving his entire sword from one side to the other.

On feints, Docciolini says some suggest their use, but he advises otherwise. The feint is a "pretend" attack, which if seen for what it is, can lead to great danger. It is far better to attack and strike than to pretend to do so.

When facing an attack, he says those who are lacking in skill or are timid use the method of *mezzotempo*. This is when you throw a hard defense to beat aside an attack, then try to respond with one. Doccioloni says it is far better to attack in *contratempo*, at the same time as the opponent in such a way as to thrust them while remaining secure. As we saw with George Silver, not all agreed that this was an inferior form of fencing, but to most (not all) Italians, the thrust in time with the opponent's attack was seen as best.

When fencing, where should one look? Docciolini says some say the face, the body, or the hand but he refutes them all. "I disagree with all of these viewpoints. Watching their body or their face, it is difficult to discern which action they might perform. Likewise watching the hand or their sword (although less of an error) their intention cannot easily be determined."[46] He goes on to say that the fencer ought to watch the point of the opponent's sword.

When it comes to holding a dagger, he says there are two wrong ways of doing it. The first is to hold the dagger close to the chest rather than extended. Doing this prevents you from using the dagger until it is too late. Second, holding the dagger with the thumb pressed to the flat of the blade invites all manner of harm to the hand if a parry or cover is not made correctly. The same goes for holding a buckler by using the thumb to brace along the handle. While the thumb is safe from harm, the grip is not secure against strong blows.

The same harm comes to the hand when someone who uses a rapier and cape holds it without wrapping it around their hand. By just holding it, as he says some do, the hand is exposed to danger. And while some suggest throwing the cape at the opponent, Docciolini says it rarely works and you just end up losing your cape. In the use of the buckler, he says holding it low is not a good idea, because a thrust high causes you to defend your face and blind yourself, inviting yourself to be struck from below.

Summary

Much of Docciolini's advice was taken as the means to fence with the rapier. Later masters, while not necessarily students of Docciolini, shared the same experiences of what made good and bad fencers. Like many Italian rapier masters, he was dubious of feints, found the thrust superior to the cut, and believed a single-time counter-attack to an opponent's attack was the surest way to victory.

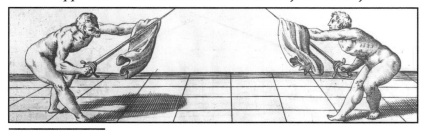

SALVATOR FABRIS

F abris' *Science of Arms* from 1606 was groundbreaking. His thoughts on the rapier were vaunted in his lifetime and well beyond. In his treatise he covers much, ranging from the basics of fencing to proper and improper ways of fighting, to methods and guards unique to him and copied by others later. On the topic of bad fencing, Fabris has plenty of advice on what not to do.

When it comes to the traditional guards of rapier, *prima, secunda, terza,* and *quarta,* Fabris shows the guards and postures that were common to Italian rapier and can be found in the contemporary works of Capo Ferro. All of these guards Fabris finds imperfect. Traditionally, a fencer put their weight on their back leg and leaned their body far back to keep themselves away from their opponent, while their hand was extended far forward to further keep the foe at bay.

Fabris believed this was common, but wrong. It was better to lean back, while bending forward. Yes, the head is exposed, but his reasoning was this: By leaning all the way back the whole body, a large target, must be defended. By leaning back, but bending the body forward, only the head is exposed and the head is a much smaller, and thus easier to guard than the whole body.

When it comes to various fencing tricks, Fabris warns against them. For those who sought to use their hand to grab the sword, "Since there are many fencers who, although armed with the sword alone, base their defense on the bare left hand rather than the sword, I see it is necessary to spend a few words on this technique ... Then I consider this way of parrying a bare hand to be a truly abysmal way to defend. But I will talk about it in order to show you how to operate against those who use it."[47] Then he proceeds to discuss many ways in which the sword can deceive the hand.

Fabris dismisses other methods of provoking an opponent's

---

47   *Salvator Fabris, Art of dueling: Salvator Fabris' Rapier Fencing Treatise of 1606. Trans. Tommaso Leoni (Highland Village, TX: Chivalry Bookshelf, 2005), 14.*

response as wasting time, and in wasting a tempo it is possible you might be struck. That meant, stomping of the foot, flinging the sword one way then the other, inviting an attack, or using weak cuts, were all hallmarks of a bad fencer. "They may be possible against inexperienced opponents, but it spells mortal danger against the experienced opponent."[48]

Of techniques, he calls out a few as bad behavior. Fencers who tuck in their arm and fling their sword were wasting time because they had to fling to strike and then draw their arm back. And while they feel they are fast; they are just giving up the weak of their sword to an opponent. "There are some who, wanting to execute a thrust, fling their sword-arm forward with force in order to give it more momentum. This is a bad technique…"[49] And like Docciolini, Fabris notes this flinging does not provide much power and takes too much time.

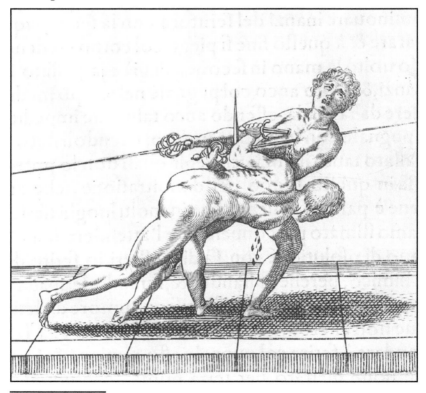

---

48   Ibid, 8-9.
49   Ibid.

Fencers who hold their arm out too straight, do have a fine defense, but they will tire and struggle because their sword is easier to gain. Fencers who keep their sword too low with the point off to the side, or fencers who try and use their left hand to fortify their blade when fighting, are all making mistakes, which Fabris says he won't belabor.

Fencers who rely on their off-hand; try to beat; or worse, try to use their sword to disarm their opponent, may find some success, but overall these are bad ideas. Fabris says these motions all take a tempo and in that tempo you can be deceived by someone who knows how to *cavazione* (disengage) and thrust.

Fabris also calls attention to fencers who do not know how to feint. These fencers make too many motions of the body and the sword to try and provoke a response, but in so doing they simply open themselves up to attack.

Fabris' second book dispenses with what can be seen as traditional Italian rapier and devises something new, proceeding instantly from the drawing of the sword and into the attack. While at first blush, this may seem rash, he spells out how to do so safely and quickly. Of his detractors he says, "Perhaps wishing to palliate their own skill, these fine gentlemen would have made an effort to refute these techniques and hide behind the commonplace."[50]

Fabris also describes the characteristics of what might be seen as bad fencers in the form of either a rash and angry opponent or a cold-blooded rational one. Both were making a mistake in his view. The hot-tempered opponent will easily be provoked into an attack out of measure or out of tempo and can thus be hit. Conversely, the cool-headed opponent who waits in a guard can be defeated by closing the distance and attacking firmly where he is open, taking care not to fall for any *contratempo* trick of his or using a proper feint to disorder him.

Summary

Fabris's thoughts are the most detailed we have on rapier and they are rather even-handed. Fabris

---

50   *Ibid. 163.*

notes the behaviors of other fencers and says that some of their bad behaviors can work! But they will not work against someone who has mastered the art of fencing as he has. He lays out a rational case as to why his method and his variations on guards and techniques are superior to others.

Overall, what he calls bad fencing is anything that wastes tempo, a recurrent theme amongst many masters. In any wasted tempo you can be attacked and Fabris used that as a way to explain the dangers and even the advantages of bad fencing. If you take too many tempo to do something, you might still succeed, but then again you might be struck. If you are aware of someone else taking too many tempo, then Fabris is confident you can easily strike them, and therein lies his advice on bad fencing. Since bad fencing exists, understand that and know how to defeat it through proper use of measure and tempo.

RIDOLFO CAPO FERRO

R idolfo Capo Ferro's work, *Great Representation of the Art and Use of Fencing,* was published in 1610 and is a good foundation for learning what the dominant style of Italian fencing looked like. His guards, attacks, feints, and techniques are what we come to expect when we think of 17th century rapier fencing. When Fabris spoke of guards that others were using that he found faulty, he was referring to the guards seen in Capo Ferro, though he was not specifically writing about him.

But what ills did Capo Ferro see if we can imagine him as a very standard definition of an Italian rapier master?

He advises people to beware of false teaching and to practice often. He says exercise is the minister of the art of fencing. Without it you cannot learn the truth behind the art. A bad fencer was one who did not understand the nature of the art of fencing, which implicated, much to his dismay, soldiers! Meyer believed gunpowder had weakened the art of fencing, and writing forty years later, Capo Ferro agrees.

Capo Ferro thought others were defining tempo incorrectly. He said some scholars falsely believed that a tempo was only the motion of the opponent's sword and body. Capo Ferro believed a lack of practice had led to this falsehood. In truth, tempo was your movement, the opponent's, and could also include a moment of stillness. The distinction may seem minor, but he believed that poor masters were teaching techniques without properly understanding tempo. As many other masters have noted, techniques without proper timing wont' work. Capo Ferro says you can't have proper timing unless you understand tempo completely: "[S]cholars take some wicked use by proceeding straight to the vanity of the *finte* (feint) and the *cavazioni* and … similar things of this sort."[51]

While in a guard, Capo Ferro says those who kept their head held too high or too low, limited their vision and could not see all the angles they might be attacked from. He also said while voids have their place, the head itself should not try to void attacks.

He says the sword arm should not be tucked back, a position which is nearly identical to those of Docciolini and Fabris on the matter.

Those who pass, meaning when their rear foot becomes the lead, should do so with a full step. Those who try small passes are unbalanced.

While Silver despised the Italian rapier masters, he and Capo Ferro agree on the folly of those who circle as they fence. Capo Ferro says that such circling wastes tempo; when your opponent takes time to circle, you can simply wait until they are in measure and circling and strike them as they move.

In his techniques, Capo Ferro obliquely refers to bad fencing. He shows a technique, but in the description he often says if the struck person was a practical person he could… and then he explains what could be done to counter the technique. So in a way, we see what the "unpractical" do in fencing.

---

51   Ridolfo Capo Ferro, *Italian Rapier Combat: Capo Ferro's 'Gran Simalcro,'* Ed. Jared Kirby, Trans. Jeanette Acosta-Martinez and Ramon Martinez (Barnsley, UK: Frontline Books, 2010), 40.

Summary

Capo Ferro takes many of the ideas and warnings of prior Italian rapier masters and largely agrees with them. While there are differences, some key components remain. To be a good fencer, you need to understand tempo. Holding the arm back or the point off-line is not a good way to fence. Feints have their value, but are difficult to perform.

All of this, more or less, can be found in early works, such as those of di Grassi and Capo Ferro's contemporaries, Docciolini, Giganti, and Fabris.

And like many masters, Capo Ferro worried about the state of fencing in his day and age.

FRANCESCO ALFIERI

lfieri was the master of arms at the Accademia Delia in
Padua, a university town since 1222 and still one today.
There he wrote his book, *On Fencing*, in 1640. His treatise
carries on the traditions of Italian rapier fencing seen in the
works of Giganti, Fabris, and Capo Ferro. He is certainly not
identical to any of them, even in his criticisms, but overall there
are themes to be found, such as a preference of the thrust and
single-time actions when possible.

He calls out the fencing community as a whole in his address
to the reader, "The numbers of fencers is infinite. Few of them
are good but all of them believe themselves to be the best."[52]

He then presents the readers with a tantalizing promise to
reveal a new guard, never before seen, that is superior to the four
standard rapier guards: *prima, secunda, terza,* and *quarta.* His
guard is *guardia mista,* which lies between *terza* and *quarta.*

Alfieri has specific criticisms toward Capo Ferro. When it
comes to guards, Capo Ferro preferred terza and explains the
weakness of *prima* and *secunda.* Alfieri agrees, but believes

---

52   *Francesco Ferdinando Alfieri, La Scherma: The Art of Fencing,
Trans. and ed. Caroline Stewart, Phil Marshall and Piermarco Terminiello
(San Bernardino: Vulpes, 2017)., 11.*

the old master overstated his case. Because Alfieri has his own preferred guard, he spends time explaining the strengths and weaknesses of the others as well as what other masters thought about them.

He says some masters (and likely he means Capo Ferro) believe the *prima* and *secunda* guards extended the blade too far forward and were too fatiguing and worse, that the blade could be easily found and gained by an opponent. Alfieri disagrees and says in the tempo it takes for an opponent to move into measure and seek the blade, they could be struck. Yes, *prima* and *secunda* have their issues but they aren't entirely useless.

Of the guards *terza* and *quarta*, he says both are strong but often used poorly. Many fencers held their hand low and bent their wrist, so that the blade pointed at the opponent's place, almost in a V shape. This was folly because for the thrust to be launched, the hand must raise and straighten and in that tempo you could be attacked.

On the positioning of the bodies, Alfieri says the Spanish masters who advise upright fencing were wrong in their opinions that it was safer. He says that the upright stance was more natural, but slow to lunge, slow to recover, and left too much of the body open to being attacked. Leaning forward was much better to lunge from, but he cautions not to overdo it.

Also, on the topic of Spanish masters, they advised circling and Alfieri says it's not a good idea because they are disordered on the attack because they have no line to defend or work from. "Many people… fall into a number of errors by taking themselves to the other extreme, forming a very forced posture with too wide a step, and curling themselves up so much that they seem little short of doubled up on themselves."[53] This may or may not be a reference to some of Fabris' compact guards. It's hard to say because Alfieri praises Fabris as one of the greatest additions to the art of fencing.

Disengaging the rapier from one side of an opponent's blade to another is called a *cavazione*. This technique is common among the rapier treatises, but Alfieri says some criticize it and say it is

---

53   *Ibid.* 27.

either used out of measure and therefore has no value, or it is used too closely to the opponent and provides a tempo for them to strike you. Alfieri agrees, but if you thrust while you conduct the *cavazione*, then no tempo is lost and the opponent is hit.

Rapier masters are often divided about the feint, noting that it is valuable, but if done poorly it leads to trouble. Alfieri agrees and says feints are of profound use, but only if they are performed in such a way as to force an opponent's response. How not to feint would be to try and feint a cut and then thrust. He says that takes far too much time and it is better to feint a thrust one place and land it in another.

The *contratempo*, having your enemy strike first but hitting him with a counter, is another technique with which Alfieri agrees with other rapier masters, but with the caviat that while it's artful it's hard to do. He says Fallopia and Viggiani, two fencers from the late 1500s, suggested waiting patiently in guard to perform such actions or perhaps a parry. He says this is not a good idea because it gives all the initiative to the opponent and if your response is wrong, then you will be wounded. He says even in fencing schools under ideal conditions, those who wait and try to react often react wrongly. It is far better to take the initiative when possible.

On the nature of cuts, most rapier masters believe the thrusts superior to the cut. Alferi agrees in principle, but once again calls out Capo Ferro for misunderstanding the value of cuts. There are times when it is appropriate to cut and he says it can wound just as grievously as a thrust. That said, cuts are slower and one should not try them while entering into the measure of an opponent.

Lunging can present problems. Alfieri says some fencers lunge so far as to nearly throw themselves onto the floor. This gives great range but has too much risk because the recovery time is so long. As he puts it, "An opponent who does not save himself in the attack is lost."[54]

When fencing, he disagrees with those who believe staring at an opponent's eyes is a good idea. The eyes betray nothing while

---

54   *Ibid.* 71.

the hand and point of his sword reveals the true danger. On the other hand, when lunging, he says some turn their heads, and this denies the use of the eyes altogether. An unwise idea!

He describes poor fencers and ways to defeat them. Those who say courage and strength alone are all that is needed in fencing are wrong in his view. And he counters their usual refrain. Those who believed courage and valor alone can win the day cite a novice (with great courage) defeating a master. "These people who have such strange ideas in their heads, deserve to be pitied more than they merit a response."[55]

But he does respond! Alfieri affirms that an untrained fencer could kill a master. These things happen rarely, but when they do everyone talks about it. When a master kills an untrained fencer, which happens all the time, no one bothers to mention it.

The wild fighter makes many mistakes, takes many tempo, and is ignorant of measure. To defeat them he says one should wait and thrust with a firm-footed lunge as they blindly come into measure. These wild fighters can be noted for their wild eyes and disregard for guards or measure.

Related to the wild fighter is the choleric one. These fencers are angry and will be jerky in their motions. They are impatient and will attack. Their attack is perhaps not as reckless as that of the wild fighter, but their impetus can be used against them.

The timid fighter can be defeated by simply adding to their nervousness by performing a variety of movements. He also says what a timid fencer will do. They will take short hesitant steps. They will parry too often and fall for feints. They will retreat at the slightest provocation. Many techniques can be used against them.

The choleric fencer is the most dangerous to fence. They wait in a guard, almost lazily and look for an opportunity. Alfieri praises such men, but still says they can be defeated by attacking first and hard so they cannot perform any of their tricks in time. This is also why he says it is not wise to wait in guard and try to counter-fight. While it is possible, and such men should be praised, few can do it safely and Alfieri believes his more aggressive style is better.

---

55   *Ibid. 14.*

He provides more advice on the strong, weak, short, and tall fencers, but offers few criticisms and more advice on how best to use what physical talents you have.

Summary

Alfieri claims to introduce some revolutionary ideas to the art of fencing, namely a guard. However, a close look finds him well within the pantheon of Capo Ferro, Fabris, and Giganti, even when he is being critical. And he is critical, calling out many bad behaviors and what others thought was good advice, but was in fact bad. He also cites examples of techniques some masters favored, but he does not.

His view on "types" of fencers is a clear-cut reveal for us on what he saw as the nature of bad fencing. Some of this was technique but more often it was bad behavior such as being too timid, too reckless or trying to counter-fight.

Alfieri also offers some perspective on the criticisms of other. For example, he says the prima and secunda guards do have issues, as do cuts, but not to take it too far. He says the same with stances. Overall, his critical responses are to be measured in your like and dislike for something.

Jacopo Monesi

Monesi was a Florentine fencing master in the service of the famous Medici family and had the patronage of wealthy nobles. Of bad fencing, he is a treasure trove of information because his treatise is less on "how to fence" and more on "why everyone is doing it badly." His brief treatise was published in 1640 under the title, *Objections and Admonishments on the Subject of Fencing.* His entire purpose for writing the treatise was that, although he did not find himself very gifted when it came to writing, he was overwhelmed by the prevalence and even fame of what he believed to be bad fencers. If the book of Bad Hema has a patron saint, it is undoubtedly Jacopo Monesi. Within his short treatise you will find little on technique and a great deal on what was wrong with the state of fencing in his day.

Monesi said most people were not good at fencing because they did not practice assaults. An assault is a drill or a sparring game. Too many youths were instead taking a few lessons on fencing and then deciding they had learned enough and were masters themselves. Worse, these men of high birth would not dare fence with someone of lower birth. Monesi believed this a great mistake, because a lowly man who learned the sword could be quite valiant.

Monesi bemoans the way these ambitious and arrogant youths learn the theory of fencing, but do not practice it, and so know nothing at all:

> *Actions are needed when it comes to training your body for defense and attack. This is not applied by today's youth, which is a further reason why assaults no longer take place, and students neglect to learn wielding a sword in hand well. It then follows that masters are judged and branded as inept in their craft, since they no longer produce students as they did in the past. When youngsters come together, sometimes from the schools of*

different masters in this profession, instead of putting their studies to the test, with the cloak across their shoulders, as well as with the simple sword in hand, they begin to discuss among themselves.[56]

In other words, they debated on what techniques they "would" do and how they "would" counter, but never fenced one another to find out what would really happen.

Of the fencing masters, Monesi says they are just as bad as their students, for when they fence, they do so in an academic way, in the safety and regulation of a fencing salle. He derides them for their drawn lines and mathematics and says, "But if I imagine them outside the tiled hall, that is in the streets, where confrontations most often arise, then I can't help but criticize and malign them, since it is impossible (for reasons I will explain) to put these actions into practice."[57] Like the youths who debate the theory of fencing, these masters do the same. Monesi says their techniques and clean fencing is tossed away the moment they get into a fight on the street, where they fall back to natural fencing rather than what they teach.

On the subject of targets, Monesi says other masters believe it is best to attack the right shoulder, something Docciolini agrees with. Monesi wonders why they think this and duly refutes each possible reasoning. If they attack the right shoulder because they believe it is closer, Monesi notes that the opponent's hand or even knee might be closer. If they attack the right shoulder because it vulnerable, Monesi again refutes this and says the hand and arms are far more vulnerable and accessible than the shoulder.

On the topic of measure, Monesi decries using matched weapons and a clean and open area to fence in. While such allows you to learn your measure, he says a real fight might be on an uneven, trash-strewn street, or a piazza not of your choosing,

---

56   Jacopo Monesi, *Objections and Admonishments on the Subject of Fencing. Trans. Piermarco Terminiello, In "Jacopo Monesi." Wiktenauer: A HEMA Alliance Project. Accessed 2020. https://www.wiktenauer.com/wiki/Jacopo_Monesi.."*

57   *Ibid.*

and you and your opponent are unlikely to have matched swords. The use of pre-determined swords and a pre-determined space is a poor way to learn the real fight.

As for voids, Monesi says it is foolish to try and void an attack, even if you are just backing up. The street may be uneven and you might stumble, the opponent's sword may be too long and your void fails, or you succeed at a void, but lose a tempo and thus gain nothing for it. Like the matched swords and defined fencing space, Monesi finds voids too artificial. To him, voids, matched weapons and, a flat and open area to fence in were fine for capering about a classroom, but not for fighting in earnest.

Many Italian rapier masters were dubious of feints. Monesi is even more opposed, saying such techniques are done for fun and play, but in a real fight there is only solid defense and solid attack and anything else is dangerous.

The use of a single-tempo response to an attack, or *contratempo,* was another concept Monesi said was a product of bad fencing. In theory, he said *contratempo* works, but in practice a good strong attack must be met with a solid defense, not with an attack at the same time. He said the use of such techniques were akin to dance steps with a willing partner. As was often his refrain, the *contratempo* was for play and not a real fight.

The artwork and guards of all the other masters, including well-established ones, was also a product of bad fencing. To Monesi, any guard that was not entirely natural to be in, was false. And so, any guard where the body crouches, or leans back, or is in a strained position was nonsense. There are so many bad guards that he names a few that might be considered bad, including the standard rapier guards of *prima, seconda, terza,* and *quarta,* but says these guards can only be judged by their actual use and comfort. If the body has to twist or contort to form the guard, then the guard is bad. He asserts that "guards to be employed should not be twisted or bizarre, nor overwrought with a paintbrush, nor measured with a compass, but simple and natural. In this manner the body finds itself stronger in resisting blows, and attacking when the occasion presents itself, without the manifest danger of stumbling and thereby compromising your life."[58]

His diatribe against unnatural and comfortable guards is likely a direct poke at Fabris whose artwork shows such contortions that even Fabris tells his readers that though it may not appear so, his art is drawn from life. Monesi is not convinced and has an entire chapter dedicated to such entitled, "On the so misshapen published figures of this exercise."[59] And by that, he means this:

Monesi complains that poor masters were giving their students terrible advice when it came to fighting at night when they urged students to crouch low and reach out with their sword to find the opponent's and once it is found, attack. Monesi says it was foolish to blindly search for the enemy, and instead you should throw *mandritta* (cuts from right to left) and *roversi* (cuts from left to right) in rapid succession and find the enemy that way!

Masters who train wearing a breastplate for protection or use a rod to fence with were teaching bad habits. Monesi said students will over-reach in their attacks because they are used to having to attack a breastplate and having to hit much harder than they would in real life. When it comes to the rod, the master moves too swiftly to be realistic and his strikes are not that of a sword, which will only confuse the student when they fence against an actual blade rather than a stick.

Monesi admonishes those who watch the point of the sword or face in a fight and says it is another product of bad teaching. As to where you should look, he says he will write about it another day. Does he? If so, the treatise has yet to be found.

Breaking from the tradition of most Italian rapier masters, Monesi says the cut is just as useful as the thrust. He said those who believe the thrust is faster are wrong, and he proved such in his own fencing experience. Those who believe the cut is not as fatal as a thrust are also wrong as proven by experience. Finally, Monesi notes that it is good to be able to use and defend against cuts, because in a real fight, you never know what your opponent

---

58   Ibid.
59   Ibid.

will do. Monesi maintains that it is important to learn the cut and thrust equally well.

In terms of the dagger, Monesi says those who try to learn defenses against it are fooling themselves. A real opponent will draw their dagger quickly and at close range, stabbing you long before you can employ any defense, of which he states are only for showing off in the schools.

Monesi says some masters believed the pike could deflect all blows, even that of a musketball. He is understandably dubious.

He even offers fashion advice, given as usual, in a manner to discuss bad fencing and their masters. High-heels are things you can trip over, and those who wear their hair long, are just asking to have it grabbed in a fight. Bad fencers also wear baggy clothes or giant sashes, all of which are things that can tangle them up.

Summary

Monesi's treatise is a great cry against, not the rapier as it was with George Silver, but with how the rapier was being taught. He believed all the celebrated and published masters of his day were in fact bad fencers, who spent too much time on the theory of fencing, and not on its actual, dirty practice. "In the practice of fencing, to engage someone in debate and discussion as if arguing theology (in place of conducting assaults) achieves nothing but to deny opportunities to those who desire to learn, to become excellent in practice."[60] And while many masters point out what they saw as bad fencing, Monesi outshines them all in his annoyance at others and their perversion of the art.

---

60   *Ibid.*

MIYAMOTO MUSASHI

Miyamoto Musashi is not in a lineage of European martial arts, but his own work, the *Book of the Five Rings*, written on the other side of the world, bears a quick investigation. This is because Musashi spends a delightful amount of time criticizing others, especially in what he called the *Wind Book* of his *Five Rings*. We can compare the Eastern to the Western master and their critique on others. Complaining about others is clearly a human universal.

In his youth, Musashi was a duelist wandering Tokugawa-ruled Japan and challenging others. Many years and many duels passed before he wrote a book discussing his thoughts on swordsmanship or what he called simply, "the way." His book covers techniques, but he also discusses the mental side of fencing as key. One does not work without the other. He is rather specific when pointing out what he saw as flaws in other systems at the time. Their focus on technique and technique alone was a mistake.

Musashi asserted, "The true value of sword-fencing cannot be seen within the confines of sword-fencing techniques,"[61] and "If we watch men of other schools discussing theory, and concentrating on techniques with the hands, even though they seem skillful to watch, they have not the slightest true spirit."[62]

To him, schools teaching many ways to hold the sword and many techniques to use them were not teaching what Musashi believed was the true way. "The way" involved cutting down your enemy first and foremost.

He dislikes those who grip their sword too tightly, those who advance with one foot over and over, and those who move from side to side. He believes that the hand should be pliant and the steps natural, as if walking. Here is his commentary on steps he doesn't like:

> *There are various methods of using the feet: floating foot, jumping foot, springing foot, treading foot, crow's foot, and such nimble walking methods. From the point of view of my strategy, these are all unsatisfactory. I dislike floating foot because the feet always tend to float during the fight. The Way must be trod firmly. Neither do I like jumping foot, because it encourages the habit of jumping, and a jumpy spirit. However much you jump, there is no real justification for it; so jumping is bad. Springing foot causes a springing spirit which is indecisive. Treading foot is a "waiting" method, and I especially dislike it.[63]*

Schools that exclusively used a very long katana, such as the nodachi, were limiting themselves. What if the enemy comes too close? What if the fight takes place in a cramped area?

---

61   *Miyamoto Musashi, The Book of the Five Rings, Holybooks.com, Accessed 2020. http://www.holybooks.com/wp-content/uploads/The-Book-of-Five-Rings-by-Musashi-Miyamoto.pdf.*

62   *Ibid.*

63   *Ibid.*

Schools that exclusively used the shorter sword, the wakizashi, were also making a mistake. What if the enemy was prepared and had a longer weapon? What if there were multiple opponents?

Schools that suggested cutting harder with better quality swords are also making an error. The sword should be used to cut and kill the enemy and it doesn't matter what kind of sword is being used, the cut is always the same. To cut too hard is to let your sword lead you out of position.

Schools that taught speed are similar because the opponent who is jumpy, fast, and rash also ends up out of position.

Schools that used defensive guards to wait in were also in error. Something the German tradition echoed. Musashi believes it was better to be on the attack, and while this may not always mean attacking first, you should be trying to do so to try and bend the enemy to your will rather than reacting to his.

"Of where to look, numerous masters had their opinions and so does Musashi. Some schools maintain that the eyes should be fixed on the enemy's sword. Some schools fix the eyes on the hands. Some fix the eyes on the face, and some fix the eyes on the feet, and so on. If you fix the eyes on these places your spirit can become confused and your strategy thwarted."[64]

Where then should one look? Musashi says it's better to take it all in and not fix on any one detail, lest you miss something else.

To achieve true mastery of the sword (and all martial arts), Musashi says the techniques must be simple and the objective, to cut down your enemy, be your entire focus. Practice alone achieves this and he makes several analogies. A carpenter can read on how to build something, but without days and years of practice, he will never master his skill. The same goes for the warrior and the way.

Summary

Although 17th century Japan is a long way off from Europe and its fencing traditions, some of what

---

64   *Ibid.*

Musashi writes can be seen in European treatises. The early German longsword of Liechtenauer and his disciples believed that cutting down an opponent and dominating the fight was key and they also disliked waiting in guard. Musashi is much the same. The two may be oceans of distance and time apart, but there is a similar spirit.

Monesi's desire for natural simplicity in fighting is also something Musashi valued. Monesi's numerous complaints about academic fencing and unnatural body positions and guards is something Musashi also shares a distaste for.

Monsieur L'Abbat

L'Abbat takes us into the 18th century and his treatise, *Questions about the Art of Weapons*, was first published in 1701 and translated into English in 1734 by Andrew Mahon, a fencing master as well. L'Abbat's treatise discusses the use of the small sword, the successor of the rapier.

In his preface to L'Abbot's work Mahon gives us complaints about modern masters and cites L'Abbat's advice. Mahon notes that L'Abbat said voids, passes, and lowering the body are bad ideas. Mahon agrees and then complains, "Notwithstanding which, there is a modern Master, who as soon as he had seen this Book, and the Attitudes representing volting, passing and lowering the Body, began and still continues teaching them to his Scholars, without considering how unsafe and dangerous they are, for want of the proper Opposition of the Sword when within Measure." And, "[S]ome Masters, who being more capricious than knowing, were fonder of the showy or superficial, than of the solid part of the science (of fencing)."[65]

As for L'Abbat, he mentions some of the behaviors or teachings he disagrees with.

When in guard, he says some masters have their students turn their head so their chin is over their shoulder and their face fully facing the opponent. He says this is straining and it is better to keep the eyes on the opponent, but the head not held in any uncomfortable position.

He also chides masters who are too rigid in their instructions. Some masters had their students hold their arm and sword at a fixed height when facing an opponent. A'bbat says this would be fine if all men were the same height, but since they are not, you should fix your blade's position according to how tall or short the opponent is.

Poor fencing comes from poor footwork. This may seem like common sense, but prior masters spend little ink on footwork.

---

65   *Andrew Mahan, Preface to Monsieur L'Abbat's The Art of Fencing, or the Use of the Small Sword, Project Gutenberg, Accessed 2020,* https://www.gutenberg.org/files/12135/12135-h/12135-h.htm.

L'Abbat notes that the bad fencer's front foot is pointed left or right and not in line with his knee. His attacks are defeated because his body is in a state of disorder and this lack of balance comes from poor footwork. He then gives exacting measurements of how one should stand, advance, and retreat.

L'Abbat mentions two masters, De Latouche and De Liancour, who did not like retreating because it took too many actions. He disagrees and alleges that the retreat can be performed in less time than the other masters believe.

Other masters' inferior teaching is brought up in technical examples, some of them quite subtle. On what guard to hold, one or the other, L'Abbat says some try to keep their hand between two guards. He says this just wastes time by setting up an inferior defense in hopes that the hand can move within the tempo of the opponent's attack.

Some masters believed a feint was the act of moving from the inside to the outside, and L'Abbat agreed but said De Latouche used the guard *quarte* for both the inside and outside of the opponent. De Latouche said this had no motion and made the feint easier. But L'Abbat deemed this wrong because the wrist does bend a little when moving from the inside to the outside.

The little details continue throughout his treatise. The translator, Mahon, notes that L'Abbat discouraged lowering the body, voids, and deep passes. While true, L'Abbat also shows how to perform them and when. And L'Abbat discourages many other small techniques. Some masters suggest grabbing the arm rather than the sword when disengaging, some masters suggest a disengage as a way to find the opponent's blade, some masters point their sword off to one side to invite an attack. All of these actions, L'Abbat said were wasting time and thus to be avoided.

Summary

L'Abbat specifically calls out other masters as in error. But it is clear he doesn't think all of these masters are actually all that bad. He is not insulting as was George Silver; rather, he carefully reasons why his methods are better than theirs and it revolves around two points that often combined. First, many masters suggested unsafe techniques, and second, many masters taught actions that seemed swift but in fact took too much time. Many of these complaints are over small details and you can even get a sense that L'Abbat is improving on the theories of other masers, such as Latouche and Liancour. The complaints of the translator are an added bonus since he says the dangerous behaviors from 1701 were still in practice in 1740.

Universally Bad

The masters had many opinions on what was considered artful and what was considered false, what was good and what was bad, what was safe and what was dangerous. Sometimes their opinions run directly counter to one another, but as whole, the masters were in agreement on some issues. There were concepts that nearly every master recognized as bad fencing.

A LACK OF PRACTICE

The masters agreed that those who theorized and never fenced were in danger of having no skill at all. Already, we have seen numerous masters exhorting their students to practice, and looking at a collection of other masters' words, the advice is the same.

FROM POL HAUSBUCH, MS 3227A, CIRCA 1400S:
"Also note this and know that one cannot speak and explain or write about fencing quite as simply and clearly as one can easily show and inform it with the hand. Therefore act on your judgement and consider the best of it and therein, exercise the bulk of that yourself in play which you think is of the best in earnest. Because practice is better than empty art, for practice is fully sufficient without art but art is not fully sufficient without practice."[66]
We note also the following: "And have the highest righteous fencer, in your mind's eye. So that he may protect you in your art. And practice your art for emergencies in the right way. And not for nothing or out of foolishness. So, you may succeed always. Because a fencer is a good and righteous man. Fencing has been invented to be seriously practiced and in good real grace."[67]

VADI, CIRCA 1482: *"One who does not practice will not parry well."*[68]

MONTE, 1509: *Has a whole chapter on how you cannot learn fighting from words alone.*

MANCIOLINO IN 1531: *"Therefore he who does not take delight in stepping in tempo and the way in which I will teach (and have taught), will enjoy neither grace nor victory in his fencing."*[69]

MAROZZO IN 1536: *"And still I say to you, that when you have made the examination and given*

---

66   Pol Hausbuch (MS 3227a), Trans. Michael Chidester, Wiktenauer: A HEMA Alliance Project, Accessed 2020, https://www.wiktenauer.com/wiki/Pol_Hausbuch_(MS_3227a).
67   Ibid.
68   Windsor, Veni Vidi Vici, 97.
69   Tom Leoni, The Complete Renaissance Swordsman: A Guide to the Use of All Manner of Weapons: Antonio Manciolino's Opera Nova (1531), (Wheaton: Freelance Academy Press, 2012), 95.

them the pros and cons of what you have taught, I want you to make them practice with you several days and amend where they have failed and make good strong attacks in order that they may practice defense: Finally when you have done this, have one of your old scholars who is a good and pleasant player and have them play with said student in order to make a brotherhood one to the other."

He is contrary to other masters in that while he values practice, he suggests that students only practice with their master present and with the master's scholars, not with those outside the school.

GIGANTI IN 1606: *"To be good at this type of play, you need much practice, because it is from this that you learn to parry and strike with great agility and speed."*[70] And he goes on to tell his students that they should fence both skilled and unskilled opponents: *"If someone who knows how to thrust faced another who does not, even if he lands his point, his opponent will deliver a cut in the same tempo, and so they will both strike each other . . . It is therefore little wonder that some good fencers, facing an untutored opponent, are quite often hit. This is because they have not practiced against those who know nothing."*[71]

CAPO FERRO IN 1610: *"For one who wishes to become a perfect [fencer] it is not sufficient to only take lessons from the Master, but it is necessary that you seek to play with diverse [fencers]. Being able, you must exercise with those that know more than you..."*[72]

---

70   Tom Leoni, Venetian Rapier: Nicoletto Giganti's 1606 Rapier Fencing Curriculum (Wheaton: Freelance Academy Press, 2010), 9.

71   Giganti, The Lost Second Book, 25-26.

72   Capo Ferro, Italian Rapier Combat, 52.

> *JOSEPH SWETNAM IN 1617: "Old weapons lie rusty in a corner." He stated further that those who did not practice, and in earnest, would learn to regret it, "In their youth they think it too soon to learn, and in age too late, yet when they are wronged, they would give anything, that they were able to answer their enemy without fear or hurt, as he were as skillful as his enemy."*[73]

He also warns about fencing those who know nothing, suggesting that you should never fence a drunkard because you may hit him, and he unaware of it hits you! Worse, if you defeat a drunkard in a duel people will call you a murderer, and if he kills you they'll shrug and say what a bad fencer you were.

> *MUSASHI FROM JAPAN IN 1643: "You must train diligently."*[74]

The masters are clear that practice is necessary. What kind of practice is debatable. Marozzo warned his students to not fence those outside their own school or without a master, while Silver and Monesi bemoaned the clean and orderly fencing of the salle which they believed was too unrealistic. Disagreements aside, they all concurred that practice was necessary, not just fencing theory.

FALSE TEACHERS

The masters were all concerned with those who taught the art falsely. Some might be humble, like Vadi, and invite others to add or omit from his work, but the majority, such as Fiore, Silver, and Monesi, warn their readers to beware of other masters and their false art.

> *FIORE IN 1410: "More than anyone else, I was careful around other Master of Arms and their students."*[75]

---

73   Swetnam, "The Schoole."
74   Musashi, The Five Rings.
75   Fiore dei Liberi, Flower of Battle, 1.

POL HAUSBUCH (MS 3722A), CIRCA 1400S:
With those, people choose to procrastinate and delay themselves. As one finds according to many illegitimate masters, that say they have invented and conceived and possess for themselves from day to day some new art, better and greater. But I would like to see one that would conceive and perform just one application or one hew that does not come from Liechtenauer's art. Just that they will often mix-up and pervert an application. So, with that, they give it a new name, each according to their head. Furthermore, that they conceive wide fencing-around and parrying and often do two or three hews in place of a single hew. They will be praised by the uncomprehending just for the liveliness of it as they fiendishly arrange themselves with those beautiful parries and wide fencing-around and deliver wide and long hews slowly and sluggishly.[76]

MANCIOLINO IN 1531:
Certainly, he who reads these banners [of other masters' schools] will find they contain principles, however, these instructors, acting as wine-merchants do with their barrels, operate more monstrously than humanly. . . . I believe that it is steely greed to place in a school what is there only for one's own benefit instead of that of others. Such are the principles of the aforementioned teachers, who do nothing but sell at a price the noble plays of our art. . . . These men do not see that a blunt mind cannot be yoked alongside sharp intellect; and the Art is not a whore to be sold at a price.[77]

JERONIMO CARANZA IN 1569, whose discourses on Spanish fencing are verbose, was delightfully

---

76   *Pol Hausbuch.*

77   *Leoni, The Complete Renaissance Swordsman, 72.*

brief when he said of other masters, *"Especially in the Art we discuss, there are professors of it who are the dregs of the republic."*[78]

And few can match **GEORGE SILVER'S** vitriol toward false teachers! *"They are imperfect in their profession, their fight is false, and they are false teachers, deceivers and murderers, and to be punished accordingly . . ."*[79]

CAPO FERRO says we should not be lulled by false masters: *"[Avoid techniques] that are submerged in the abyss of dark gloomy falseness and deceitful opinions."*[80]

He went on to say that *"they are long winded and very confusing and similarly contradict themselves most of the time. It is because they do not first cast a stable foundation from these infallible and well-ordered precepts of the art."*[81]

MUSASHI IN 1643: *"They speak of 'This Dojo' and 'That Dojo.' They are looking for profit. Someone once said, 'Immature strategy is the cause of grief.' That was a true saying."*[82]

Time and again the masters warn about other masters and their duplicitous teaching, which might look good in the classroom, but in an actual duel would fail. There is some economic motivation behind this disparaging of other masters. These men were all in the same profession after the same clients. That said, the motivation was not entirely economic. Silver, for all his hatred of the Italian method of fencing, cites humanity as a cause. His was a method that would preserve your life and the false masters would only get you killed.

---

78   Koepp, (trans). "Jeronimo Sanchez de Carranza."

79   Silver, "Paradoxes of Defense."

80   Kirby, Italian Rapier Combat, 49.

81   Ibid. 50.

82   Musashi, The Five Rings.

Wild Fighters

The masters recognized there was a difference between courageous and reckless. The courageous fencer is not afraid to attack, the reckless fencer attacks even when they shouldn't. This comes from a lack of understanding of timing (tempo) and distance (measure). And while the wild fighter might make a great noise and perform great attacks, they can be defeated by one who recognizes them as more brawn than skill. Be it Liechtenauer's buffalo, Fiore's peasant, or an Italian rapier master's bestial or hot blooded man, the masters recognized this as bad fencing.

> **Manciolini in 1531:** *"Were our weapons despoiled of its proper steps, it would fall into the darkness of a serene night being orphaned of the stars. And how can white clad victory be, where gentle grace is lacking? We shan't therefore call the victor who wins by chance and throws random blows like a brutal peasant."*[83]

> **Giganti in 1606:** *"There are many who, in the salle, attack the opponent with full intent and deliver thrusts, imbrocatta and cuts without any respect to tempo, but always throwing blows with fury and vehemence. This is the kind of play that will unsettle every good fencer, which is why it is important to know what to do against it."*[84] *And he advises fighting in two tempo, dashing aside attacks and waiting for an opportunity to strike, something Capo Ferro agrees with.*

> **Capo Ferro in 1610:** *"If you encounter a brutal man who, without misura (measure) and tempo, hurls many blows at you with great impetus, you will be able to do two things,"* [85] *at which point he says to attack the opponent when he opens himself*

---

83   Leoni, The Complete Renaissance Swordsman, 95.
84   Leoni, Venetian Rapier, 24.
85   Capo Ferro, Italian Rapier Combat, 51.

up, either before he delivers a blow, or backing up and striking after he misses.

JOSEPH SWETNAM IN 1617, put it succinctly, *"He that to wrath and anger is thrall, over his wits hath no power at all."*[86]

ALFIERI IN 1640: *"Fury for the most part is disordered, and its outcome very poor."*[87]

MUSASHI IN 1643: *"If you rely on strength, when you hit the enemy's sword you will inevitably hit too hard. If you do this, your own sword will be carried along as a result."*[88]

To the masters, the angry, wild, unskilled or downright drunk opponent was one who did not understand measure and tempo. The longsword, sidesword, and rapier sources suggest that such fencers will make wide motions and their attacks can be deflected in some fashion, or the angry opponent will over-extend and miss and thus be opened up for a counter. A flurry of blows without a sense of timing is a hallmark of a bad fencer.

TIMID FIGHTERS

The opposite of the wild fighter is the one too afraid to fight. The fearful cannot learn the art. The masters suggest such people should never fight at all. Both Liechtenauer and Fiore say fencing is not for the fearful and this is echoed later by other masters.

ALFIERI IN 1640: *"The timid only think of defense."*[89]

The issue with the timid fighter is that they are waiting to be attacked and thus will be. If they were skilled, perhaps they could correctly counter, but many masters noted that those who tried

---

86   Swetnam, "The Schoole."
87   Alfieri, La Scherma, 84.
88   Musashi, The Five Rings.
89   Alfieri, La Scherma, 41.

to counter-fight had to be very good because it was hard to do. The timid fencer is not very good and susceptible to feints and hard attacks, and in general is just waiting to die.

WASTING TIME

While not all of the masters use the term tempo to discuss a moment of time, they all understood it. They may employ the German tradition of using terms like *vor, nach* and *indes*; George Silver's true and false times; or the Italian terms of tempo and *contratempo*. No matter what definition of time the masters gave, they agreed wasting it was folly.

Now, what constitutes wasting time was something they did not all agree on. The Italian rapier masters generally suggested trying to do everything in a single tempo and the German master strikes were much the same, while Fiore, Silver, Monesi, and others were all perfectly fine with two tempo actions such as a parry and riposte.

Differences aside, they all recognized a bad fencer was one who didn't understand time at all. They would use slow actions when they should use quick ones; they would wait too long when they should act. The fencer ignorant of timing was making a great mistake. The bad fencer in nearly every treatise is the one who doesn't understand timing.

Contentious Fencing

The masters were divided on some concepts and provide argument and counter-argument as to why a technique was good or bad.

CUT AND THRUST

The issue of the cut and thrust was twofold. First, which was faster? Second, which was more deadly? Di Grassi and most rapier masters side with the thrust as both faster and more deadly, while Silver and Monesi favor the cut, and some masters straddled the fence. This debate would not just take place between fencing masters but was raging during the Napoleonic Wars, where the British army believed heavy cutting sabers were fearsome and effective, while the French said the thrust from a cuirassier was more fatal and quicker to perform than a clumsy blow.

The crux was a simple matter of geometry. A cut needs to be raised then thrown. This takes two tempo. A thrust simply extends out of a guard and takes one tempo. Therefore, a thrust is faster to its target. On the surface this is true, but Silver points out that if the cutter is in a raised guard, his two tempo attack is shortened to one.

As for which was more debilitating and fatal? This was entirely anecdotal with the masters giving examples of how quickly a thrust or cut disabled an opponent depending on which they favored.

While the "cut vs thrust" debate shows up in many treatises, they are often not so dogmatic as to say it must be one or the other. Silver champions the cut but at the same time he derides schools that don't teach the thrust. Alfieri says the thrust is faster, but under the right conditions a cut can be just as quick and deadly. The masters had a habit of overstating the zeal of their opponents, believing their fellow-masters advocated only thrusting or only cutting, when more often than not they heavily favored one over the other.

FEINTING

The masters were not in unison on the feint. But even those who did approve of its use were fairly similar in how it was done wrong.

A feint done well, was masterful, but done poorly it wasted time and could get you killed. The problem was, how does a feint become effective? The masters are in rough agreement. A feint that is "sold"well will work and one that is not will fail. And for the masters who believed the feint was valid, their advice is similar.

Alfonso Falloppia, 1584, explains a bad feint succinctly, "Every time someone performs a feint against you, meet him in that first tempo. Because your enemy employs two tempos, one to feint and the other to wound, while you need only one tempo to wound."[90]

Fabris, 1606, writes, "A feint is when you show your opponent that you are attacking one target and you then attack another in the tempo of his parry." He then explains many ways to do this incorrectly, such as trying to get a reaction by stomping the foot, flinging the sword too far forward or to the side, or by lurching with the body. In every case, too much time is spent selling the feint when it should be done quickly and in a way that the feint could, if the opponent does nothing, hit its original target.

L'Abbat in 1701 gives numerous ways the feint can be done wrong, be it a double-feint or one with large body motions. In both cases he says the feint takes too much time and is more dangerous to you than the opponent. "Avoid an inconvenience into which many people fall, by uncovering themselves in endeavoring to uncover the adversary."[91]

PARRYING

The masters were divided on the issue of parrying. Was it wise to commit fully to a defense?

The German tradition believed that a parry was nothing more than chasing the blade and they had many techniques to deceive such actions. It was far better to attack and attack in a such a way that the enemy could not respond. If your opponent did manage to parry your attack you still had the initiative to try something else and were in no danger. Italian rapier masters largely agreed that parrying was opening yourself up to deception. Giganti, Fabris, and Capo Ferro, the early 17th century masters, all describe the *cavazione* (disengage) as the technique to use

---

90   Alfonso Falloppia, *New and Brief Method of Fencing, Trans. Piermarco Terminiello* (Bergamo, Italy: Printed by Comin Ventura, 1584), Accessed 2020. https://wiktenauer.com/wiki/Alfonso_Falloppia#Sword_ Alone.
91   *L'Abbat, The Art of Fencing.*

against someone who parries, and it's one of the first things they describe in their treatises.

Fiore, dei Liberi, Silver, Monesi, as well some later 17th century rapier masters such as Bruchius and L'Ange, are more welcoming of the parry. For Fiore, a parry could be done while closing the distance and using the offhand to grapple, or the parry could be a deflection used to open up the opponent. For Bruchius and L'Ange, the parry sometimes was necessary and shouldn't be entirely forsaken.

SCIENCE AND ART

While outside the scope of this book, many masters debated the nature of fencing itself. Is it an art, learned through practice? An art that in some ways is developed by our very nature? Is it akin to the Renaissance artist Michelangelo? Sure, anyone can learn to sculpt, but only Michelangelo can be Michelangelo and so truly great fencers are born as much as they are trained.

Or, is fencing actually a science in which there is a mathematical perfection to every action? Is it a science in which the fencer simply must know the math and physics behind fencing to be good at it? Leverage is leverage, length is length and tempo and measure are concepts everyone is bound by. So, if you know the science well do you also know how to fence well?

The masters debated this and often simply declared their personal art to be true whether they relied on science or not. Titles with such phrases as, the true principles, the true art, the true system, the true fight, the proper instruction, the science of, and so on were common.

What we see as science and what the masters saw as science was different. Pietro Monte was a late 15th century swordsman, fencing-master and soldier. His collections on fighting theory were in his day and age considered the pinnacle of science and art. Indeed, he gives plenty of practical advice on combat, such as what blows are best, how armor is to be worn, wrestling techniques and so on. He also spends an inordinate amount of time discussing Galen's four humors and how they apply to potential soldiers. He lectures that where a person is born affects their humors and that this is well-known when it comes to animals, such as horses. Monte goes on to explain how a man's primary humor creates a temperament- sanguine, choleric, melancholic or phlegmatic. These temperaments determine their abilities. He writes of this with the same level of certainty we would write about gravity existing. To us, the idea that the four humors, our place of birth and skin pallor is the primary determinant of fencing ability would be highly suspect, but to the masters, like Monte, it was science![92]

VOIDS

There are different types of voids and some are almost universally acclaimed. If an opponent cuts at your leg, pull your leg back and strike them at the same time. This technique shows up in Fiore dei Liberi's work of 1410 and was still accepted as good fencing into the 19th century with the slipping of the leg.

If an opponent is barely in measure and attacks and you step back so they miss, then return with a cut. There is no real contention there either. However, in the rapier treatises there is a void in which you circle your rear foot behind your lead, thus taking your body off the line. At the same time you strike your opponent. The same can be done by taking the lead foot well off line while both dodging an attack and thrusting at your opponent.

This void of the body was a contentious technique along the same lines as the feint. Monesi notes that voids only work in a clean and academic setting. Other masters were not quite as vociferous in their complaints but agreed that voids of the body could be dangerous if not done correctly.

Di Grassi, Giganti, Capo Ferro, Fabris, Alfieri, and many more rapier masters give numerous ways to perform the void with names such as *girata* and *inquartata*. Yet, they also describe counters to these techniques. Still other masters warn against using them in anything outside the salle.

---

92   Monte, *Collectanea*, 52-61.

WAITING IN GUARD

Should a skilled fencer wait for his opponent to attack and then respond? The masters are divided.

The German tradition from the 1400s; Monte from 1509, Musashi from Japan; and many 17th century Italian rapier masters such as Capo Ferro, Fabris and Alfieri believe waiting in guard and responding is too risky. While the weapons and methods of the Germans of the 15th century and Italians of the 17th century are different, their proponents both noted that by waiting you give the opponent the opportunity to attack. If you are skilled, perhaps you will respond correctly with a deflection or single-tempo counter. Yet, more often than not, you are going to be wounded as you cannot guess the opponent's intention or measure correctly.

On the other side of the debate, Fiore dei Liberi from the 15th century and Giganti from the 17th both note the value of waiting. Both believe by offering an invitation you could lure the opponent into attacking. The key is deception. Can you lure your opponent into attacking what you are presenting? Can you respond the correct way?

Part of this riddle is solved by creating attractive openings and knowing fully on how to respond. Giganti notes that when fencing a superior opponent invitations may be the only way to win, and that the more deceptive opponent will win. While Meyer discourages waiting in guard, he also notes that a person who waits is either a fool or a master.

Modern Practice

What can we learn today from the admonitions and complaints of the masters? The masters sometimes contradicted themselves. The masters were using different weapons in different contexts. Could good and bad all be subjective save for a handful of universal cases? No. Even when the masters directly contradict one another, we should take them at face value and try to apply it to our own art. HEMA is about is re-creating the martial arts of the past, and sometimes that means pursuing historically bad HEMA to understand why the masters' methods worked for them and under what conditions.

For example, Fiore has no issue waiting in a guard and reacting, while the German masters advise against it. Manciolino and di Grassi argue opposite points on how heavy a training weapon should be. Monesi contradicts nearly everything Docciolini writes. Silver tells us the methods of the Italian masters are so bad that we're better off just running onto the point of a sword rather than learning from them. The complaints and contradictions can inform us!

John Patterson and I are founders of the Phoenix Society of Historical Swordsmanship. Between us we have won many tournaments and have had many students who have won tournaments. Our students have grown up to become teachers. Kyle Griswold (one of ours) and his wife Brittany have created their own school, Mordhau, with their own award-winning students. Shane Gibson teaches students in Cottonwood. I expect more of our students will go on to be running their own schools.

John and I have worked with teenagers, adults, and the elderly. We have taught outdoors, in cramped indoor conditions, in mud, in desert heat, and even in snow, and more recently in a nice gym.

For over ten years we have been teaching HEMA to others, and by trade I am a history teacher and have taught for twenty years. We have taught hand-to-hand combat; the use of daggers, rapiers, sidewords, longswords, dussacks, sabers, spears, and pole-axes; how to fight in armor and without; and continually dabble with other weapons to expand our understanding of martial arts. We have researched the source material from many disciplines, and I've gone on to write about HEMA to provide insight and research for the community.

What does it all mean? It means we have worked with a diverse number of students and have been able to make them better fencers. Some went on to do well in tournaments, some went on to teach others, some came to us barely able to walk, and are now in great physical shape. Some found themselves drawn to us by a particular weapon but went on to excel with another. Some didn't come to us to be competitive but wanted to know history, learn swordsmanship, and become competent. This they achieved.

Through it all, John and I have seen and made common mistakes that all of us must deal with on our mutual journey of understanding HEMA. I asked John and the other club members, from instructors to students, to take a single topic on what they saw as bad habits and what we did to fix them. If you are a newer student to HEMA or even an experienced martial artist, pay attention to the mistakes and errors of today, as seen through the eyes of teachers and students alike.

Richard Marsden

Sources

A mistake I see is a lack of familiarity with the sources, more so in newer students than those who have been practicing HEMA for a few years. One of my early mistakes was assuming that everyone interested in Historical European Martial Arts would gleefully read the ancient treatises. I was wrong. The reason for this is simple. Students don't read the source material because they don't have to.

Newer students have instructors to teach them and the instructors have already read and interpreted the source material. While this is acceptable for a while, there comes a time when a student has to read the material they purport to be using. Failure to do this means the student may miss something, and they will certainly struggle to teach others when they haven't fully delved into the actual words of the master they are emulating.

And this learning of the source material can be as beneficial to the teacher as to the student. I remember one particular play I was teaching from Fiore dei Liberi's *Flower of Battle*, and I dutifully pointed it out in the book. My method was a bit clumsy, but I said, "Well, not everything in the source is easy to do." At which point one of my students, peering hard, used the source material to do the technique a different way.

"What if we did it like this?" he asked. He also noted that his method fit the image and the text as all good interpretations should.

And he was right! As the teacher, I had learned from the student, who had learned from looking at the source material. This was good for all. Had he never been exposed to the source material, he would still have gone on to be a great fencer, but not as great as he has become because he would have learned an inferior technique from me. And that's the thing to remember: The sources make *all* of us better at HEMA.

For more senior students and instructors, a mistake I see is the lack of reading of sources outside their discipline. While I am a bit of a jack-of-all-trades, I believe even someone dedicated to one weapon and one source should read contemporary source material. If for no other reason, it helps you to know what others were doing at the time so that your own art makes sense in its proper context.

Fiore and the Liechtenauer tradition are prime examples. They come from the same time period. Both teach the use of the longsword and other weapons. One rejects the method of the other. In particular, is it a good idea to wait in a guard and deflect? Why does Fiore do it? Why does the Liechtenauer tradition oppose it? Are there exceptions? Only by reading the source material from each can a deep answer be discovered. As in a debate, if you only know what your side proposes, you will struggle to counter the opinions of the other side because you don't really understand what they want. The same goes for source material! Know your source well, but also read up on source material that opposes or criticizes the techniques you use.

The sources give us context, and many who are new to HEMA miss out on that. I also don't blame them. If they are learning to spar and fence for fun and fence in tournaments, why know the context of their source material? However, as a student progresses, I believe it's important to know the context of their source material. It may explain what works and what doesn't in a historical setting. For example, the Polish saber system avoids thrusts and relies on the cross-cut. Why? Because in duels among Polish men they were trying to wound one another and not kill. And so this explains why in trying to re-create a Polish duel, it is best to not allow thrusts to stay true to the art's intended purpose. Without the sources, you won't be able to know some of the reasoning behind the techniques which may be contextual as much as practical.

And finally, the sources give us HEMA. It is simply too easy to dispense with them and for students to learn what works best in sparring or a tournament or even in a drill and forget why we are here in the first place. HEMA is a collection of lost arts being revived today; there is nothing to say those arts couldn't be lost again. It is a mistake to forget them and a worse mistake to never learn them at all.

How can you get your students to read? Be sure to use the source material in class so they see the value of it. Also, if you have a particularly dedicated student, buy them a book! While the internet has plenty of free resources, a book in hand may be just the thing they need to start understanding the sources on their own.

JOHN PATTERSON

MEASURE AND TEMPO

One of the most common mistakes I see among HEMA practitioners (particularly new ones) is attacking out of measure and wasting tempo. This leads to wasted actions and recklessly brings them into danger.

The temptation to act out of measure, or at the very edge, is often a natural response when you want to keep your opponent as far away as possible. The result is that you might use just the tip of the weapon and your attacks can miss entirely. Perhaps you will get lucky and your opponent will step into your strike, fling his hands into it, or move his weapon in the way. But that is not a sound strategy.

The Italian rapier treatises are very explicit about distance and time, and I find that measure and tempo are useful tools for all types of HEMA practices. Tempo is a moment in a fight. It's not a hard measure of time but an opportunity to act. Every movement is taking a tempo, even if it is very small. Your opponent can act in these tempos. A wasted movement is also a tempo.

Measure can be defined as the shortest distance between two fighters and can be split into four categories. A student should be able to understand and explain these categories:

Out of measure: You can't reach your opponent with an attack, even with a passing step or a long lunge. As long as your opponent is out of measure, your tempo isn't that important.

Long: You have to take a full or passing step or a long lunge to reach your opponent, but you can accomplish this is one tempo, albeit a large one. You have time to process and react.

Short: You can reach your opponent with a simple step or body movement. However, if you miss, your opponent can counter quickly in the following tempo. There is less time to react and respond.

Close: You can grab your opponent without any footwork, just by moving your arms. There is very little time to react, and mistakes can be punished almost too quickly for you to process. Almost all knife fighting happens at this distance.

Some masters suggest staying one step out of measure and forcing your opponent to close that distance, giving you more time to react. Some suggest bringing the fight to the opponent, forcing them to respond. Consult your sources to see how the master you are studying treated tempo and measure.

DRILLS:

Here are some drills you can use to teach proper measure and tempo. If your student will be cutting (rather than thrusting), it can be helpful to put two bright tape lines on the area of the weapon you want the student to strike with. This will help with the natural and common impulse to strike with the very tip of the blade. Also, this is a good time to work on maintaining structure and controlling the movement and power of the weapon.

DRILL 1: Start the student at the end of a successful strike, whether it's a lunge or cut. Allow them to position themselves. Then have them notice the distance between their feet and their opponent's lead foot. Usually, they are surprised at how short the distance is. Then have them keep the weapon in contact and rewind the footwork they would have used for the strike. Again, point out the distance between their feet and their opponent's lead foot. This is the proper measure. Next, have the student withdraw the weapon to a starting position, as if at the beginning of the attack. Have them play out the attack forwards and backwards, adjusting their structure and technique until they have a good feeling for the proper distance. With practice, the student will understand their measure and what range is best to strike an opponent.

DRILL 2: The student sits in a guard, ready to strike. The instructor then approaches slowly. When the student feels they are in measure to strike, they will say "stop," then throw the attack and pause. Often, the student will be out of measure and not reach the target. Adjust and repeat until the student is consistently successful.

DRILL 3: This drill is similar to the one above but with both participants moving. This is a good drill for students to work on together. Eventually, you can have them work on intentionally attacking at different measures. With practice the students will get a feel for what is too far away, what is too close, and how to interpret measure when both parties are moving.

DRILL 4: Fence with the student. As the instructor, keep a good distance but don't move too fast. You want the student to attack you and if they are good with their measure, they will hit you. When the student misses their attack, let it just catch air without parrying or countering. Call a halt and then discuss the distance and the lost tempo.

TRAINING GAMES:

Here are some games we use to help our students improve their techniques. Combined with drills and sparring the students rapidly come to an understanding of measure and tempo.

GAME 1: In our club, we usually play this game with single sticks. It is called "wiff." One person has a single-stick and the other does not. The goal of the person with the stick is to hit the other person on the head. The goal of the person without the stick is to get the other person to swing at them and miss. The attacker is stationary and can take an advance or lunge only when they are ready to attack. They only get one attack. The defender has to get close enough to draw out the attack, but not so close that they can't escape it. Both students learn about measure playing the game.

GAME 2: This is Level 2 of "wiff." Each fighter has a stick, and there are no movement restrictions. To win you must hit your opponent on the head or have your opponent swing at you and miss. There is no parrying, only avoiding the attack and attacking. As before, a student is only able to launch a single attack. This game takes the lesson of measure and combines it with tempo. They need to find the right time to attack as well as the right distance.

Measure and tempo will undoubtedly be the first hurdle a student has to overcome. It was for me! Games, drills and practice will give you the experience necessary to make measure and tempo intuitive. We have had students who came to us and would swing wildly out of measure or walk into thrusts, but after only a few weeks of training they rapidly get a sense of their measure and tempo as well as that of their opponent.

Frederic David

Ignoring the Basics

When I started HEMA, I can't count how many times I went to look for a new technique in the sources or in a video and thought, "Great, I am going to do that at the next practice!" just to find out that it wouldn't work. I was also finding that techniques I could do in drills would not work in sparring. The most useful piece of advice that has helped me sort this out is in the preface section of Ms. 3227a - before the fancy techniques. "Also know when it comes to fencing one against another, he should be well aware of the adversary's steps and be secure and well-trained with his own, just as if he were standing on scales."[93]

I often see myself and people I train with missing that advice when fighting and ending up off balance or even with one foot in the air (often the back foot after an offensive action, trying to over-reach). This results in inefficient follow-up actions, whether it be a parry, a continuation of the offensive action, or the next necessary step.

"Also, you need control and measure in your fencing as it is appropriate, and you should not step too far, forwards or backwards, so that you can still step as appropriate, and you don't lose time while recovering from your first step."[94]

---

93   *Liechtenauer, Zettel.*
94   *Ibid.*

I have found when coaching people or when trying to fix my own problems, this is one of the most common reasons why some seemingly appropriate techniques or well thought tactical plans end up not working. The lack of balance results in a slow or inappropriate execution: Right technique but wrong timing and footwork.

I have found when people start there are often two types of people when it comes to steps: the ones like me who over-step and the shy fencer who has tiny steps. Perhaps this is why we are told two things, "Also, it is often advisable to do two small steps instead of one long step, and often it is necessary that one has to do a little run with many small steps."[95] And secondly, "Also doing an explosive step or a jump is often necessary."

The quotes may sound somewhat contrary, but the word *often* is used, and I believe it implies that there are situations where either is appropriate.

"That which one intends to execute for fun or in earnest, should be made strange and confusing to the eyes, so that the adversary will not notice what is going on."

One of my instructors once told me fencers are particularly good if they can do the same technique over and over, hitting their opponent (and not getting hit themself). He then proceeded to demonstrate that and kept hitting me on the head with a simple *oberhau* after telling me he would do that. The same can also be done with much more complex techniques, but I believe the key here is to manipulate the opponent so that they realize only too late what you are doing. I often find myself and other HEMA practitioners getting frustrated once they have some technique working for a while but then their opponents start figuring it out and the technique works less and less. Often, practitioners end up looking into other techniques, but I would also suggest trying to develop other ways to set up the same technique. These can include the use of measure, tempo, different attitudes (more aggressive or defensive, for example), or deceptions by initially showing intent of doing something else. Use the basics to try your techniques differently. This could probably be the subject

---

95   Ibid.

of an entire book of its own!

"[S]erious fencing moves simply, directly and straight, without any hesitation and pause, just like a string or like everything would be exactly measured and calculated."[96]

I realized this issue when watching some of my fighting videos in slow motion and have been noticing it more and more in others. I find that when launching a direct attack, I perform some slight but significant motion when the opponent starts their (expected) reaction. Typically, this is a hand motion for a parry or counterattack. Especially when attacking with a thrust, I have found that this slight motion on my part when my opponent reacts makes me miss my first attack. At the same time, it increases my risk of getting hit as my first intention fails. I believe the cause of the "hesitation and pause" can be quite different between fencers, whether it is fear of getting hit, fear of missing, or in my case, over-reaction to the opponent's reactions.

To improve, I need to practice the basic advice of the masters to not hesitate or pause: "Practice is better than art; your practice may very well be useful without art, but your art is useless without practice."[97]

And so, my advice is to remember the basics of good footwork and good timing. Be self-reflective on the basics. Even if you are very advanced, look at yourself and ask, "Do I need to go back to the basics so I can improve elsewhere?"

---

96   *Pol Hausbuch, MS 3227a.*
97   *Liechtenauer, Zettel.*

James Harvey Grant

Passive Sparring

A mistake I encounter in newer students is when they approach sparring passively rather than actively, that is to say, most exchanges are approached without a plan in mind. They lack not just a decision tree but also any plan at all. They are passive observers to the sparring match they are in!

Approaching any exchange without some action in mind can lead to a few problems. First and foremost, it often means that the opponent will have the opportunity to make the first move. This is something some sources, especially in the Liechtenauer tradition, explicitly state should be avoided. In the case of other sources such as Fiore's *Flower of Battle*, waiting in guard is used to set up a play. In both cases, the fencer has the initiative whether they are attacking or countering. New fencers often lack any sense of initiative and once they spar, they wait, swipe at swords, or with great hesitation launch attacks out of measure. A student who is passively waiting and reacting to the actions of their opponent is in great danger, and this warning can be found in the writings of fencing masters throughout HEMA, from longsword to rapier.

How do we make students more active in their sparring? Having them work on drills on specific plays creates an active mindset; the objectives are set by the drill and repeated until the student can understand the play in that setting. Students can use drills to quickly learn guards, footwork, and enough plays to become comfortable with the core material of a source. The next step is to get them to take what they learned from a drill setting to that of sparring.

It is important to review the source with the students. Most offer instructions and advice on what a guard can do, what it counters, and what foils it. This reading can be done as a group, looking at passages, followed by drills and demonstrations of the described actions. By following the source material, students can be prepared to create their own plans of action when they are sparring, actively improving their understanding of the material while they fence.

Even with this instruction, it can be apparent when watching sparring that a student has no plan in mind. As I have become fond of doing when coaching sparring, it is always worthwhile to ask students what their plan is going into the exchange regardless of their performance. This can be helpful for fine-tuning techniques if a chosen play is not working as expected or is being misapplied. It is also useful for confirming that the student's interpretation of the play looks correct. However, if the answer is that there was no plan to begin with, the solution is to encourage a more active practice.

One way to show students how to do this is to create a sparring drill where they face an opponent with a defined move set, anything from a single attack to a specific play. Before the exchange, ask the student to articulate a plan to thwart the given actions of the opponent using a play from whatever source is being utilized. Encourage students to try this several times, trying as many plans as they can formulate based on their knowledge of the source material. This can also be used to introduce new plays they may not know yet or refine and put into action the ones they do know.

The sources that we study tend to agree that opponents should be approached decisively, which requires at least an initial plan in mind. This should not be complicated; it can be as simple as choosing an opening attack and pursuing it.

Clearly, not every plan will always end in success, and the plan may need to change to adapt to the actions of the opponent. That is where the decision tree comes in handy.

Shane Gibson

The Dreaded Double

I think we can all agree that double hits are the worst thing in HEMA right? Simultaneous hits, double kills, or just "doubles" mar good fencing. It's understandable why they occur, and often it can be difficult to avoid them. Fencing happens fast and it can be challenging to read the actions of your opponent. When you attack you often create an opening at the same time that leaves you vulnerable. Sometimes people fight suicidally. Picture this: Two longsword fencers approach each other. Fencer A enters into range and launches a strike to the head of fencer B. Fencer B, being the suicidal maniac he is, ignores that strike and launches a strike at Fencer A's leg. We normally rule this a double hit and chastise Fencer B for being suicidal, but the fact remains that fencer A lost a leg in order to "win" that fight, and it's hard to say what he could have done better.

Most double hits aren't this lopsided, but ultimately if you're getting hit, you're not defending properly. When newer students begin sparring I commonly see them reflexively leave a bind to strike a lower target, thus giving up their head. I try to remind them that the word fencing comes from the word defense. For me this means that if you want to have some skill with a sword you need to be able to attack your opponent without being harmed yourself. Prioritizing defense doesn't mean you should just wait for your opponent to act and try to defend. I believe most fencing masters warn you against this kind of thing. In the Liechtenauer tradition there is a great line that goes something like: "He who chases the sword deserves little joy in his art." I've always interpreted this to mean that your fencing will not be very dynamic or artful, and you will probably end up getting hit before you can successfully launch an attack of your own. For me, prioritizing defense is a mindset in which I try to respect my opponent's sword as if it were sharp, and not commit to strikes that obviously leave me in dangerous positions.

So, in terms of techniques what can we do to minimize doubles? If we look to the sources, we have some principles and techniques such as single-time counterattacks, controlling the opponent's sword while attacking, and feinting/deceiving opponents in order to land a blow while not getting struck in the same tempo or shortly after. Single-time counterattacks (such as the *meisterhauwen* or "mastercuts" from the Liechtenauer tradition) can be employed to strike your opponent in such a way that protects you from a simultaneous strike. These are relatively high level techniques and can be difficult to perform successfully. Even worse, many people end up doubling when trying to perform them. But these techniques are clearly praised in some sources, so if you can pull them off, you're the man!

Controlling your opponent's blade is a more generic principle of ensuring that your opponent cannot strike you while you set up your own attack. Sticking with the Liechtenauer tradition we have concepts such as *winden* and *absetzen* which can be employed to control your opponent's blade to keep you safe while using angles, leverage, and timing to strike your opponent.

More broadly we have grappling and blade grabbing which can be used to literally control your opponent or his weapon in order to disable him from attacking you while you land your own blow. Feinting and otherwise deceiving your opponent relies on drawing some type of reaction from your opponent that you can then capitalize on. You could feint a blow to one opening to draw a parry and then attack a different opening, or you could lower your blade and lean your head forward inviting an attack which you can then counter. The sources are full of plays like this.

Many of these principles and techniques you find in the sources are effective against a skilled opponent playing the same game as you, but what about suicidal fencer B? There are more common principles and techniques we should keep in mind when fencing (especially with a new or unknown opponent). Before launching a committed attack, you should feel your opponent out. Try to gauge the reactions and skill levels of your opponent. You could launch a strike (without over committing) slightly out of range, or put your point in your opponent's face, or chamber a heavy blow, or even just stomp on the ground to see how your opponent reacts. You can use movement and distance to draw your opponent out of a threatening guard or bait them to commit to a strike while you're just out of range, or otherwise gain some advantage. In general, keep in mind that not all aspects of fencing are done with the sword.

Truthfully, you're still going to suffer double hits now and then, and that's okay. Thankfully we're not using sharp swords in earnest fighting, so it's not that consequential. Hopefully, these thoughts help you conceptualize the occurrence of doubles in your fencing, and allow you to better find solutions in whatever sources you study.

KATIE MORIN

DECISION TREES

Something I struggled with when I started practicing HEMA was a lack of a decision tree. My very first lesson covered the grappling section of Fiore dei Liberi's, the *Flower of Battle*. The holds, pushes, and strikes at the beginning of the manual are the foundation for many subsequent plays. I was highly motivated to master and execute these plays. I soon easily accomplished grapples in a drill and begun using them in sparring. Initially I was successful, and the excitement of success pushed me to grapple more often. I knew I could do it, so I tried to force a grapple in nearly every encounter.

But soon my opponents were able to thwart my attempts! When I failed, I blamed my strength and technique. I told myself I must have compromised my structure or that I needed to use more power. In truth the issue was that I had fallen into the common new-fighter pattern of finding one thing that worked and using it all the time, regardless of the situation.

When the grappling technique I was using stopped working, I didn't just pick a new piece to practice, for grappling is a big part of Fiore's manual and I told myself that I should be able to do this! I had the urge to correct each failure, wanting to keep practicing until the play worked and succeeded all of the time!

I would ask my (very patient and supportive) club members to drill these plays with me until I perfected the form and timing, then resume my efforts in sparring.

No matter the situation, I always internalized failed plays as a lack of my abilities. This cycle continued until my friend and coach, Frederick David, pointed out that success in fencing has a lot more factors to it than structure and form. I had to consider other factors, or I wouldn't find success, such as observing what my opponent is doing. I began assessing my timing, attack patterns, footwork, and overall planning. All of these had a significant impact on whether I would land an attack or not. I started making observations about my opponent and their fighting style, which informed me if a grapple was the "right" move to make or not. Did they run away? Were they three times my size? Do they fly off the bind all of the time?

I also needed to consider the information I was giving to my opponent. I had been using repetitive and straight-forward footwork and I always made a strong cut to seek the bind. I wasn't varying my attack pattern enough and I tried to close the distance without considering what my opponent was doing. The sheer predictability of training one type of attack was damaging to me. My opponents had figured me out and it was time to change.

I started to create decision trees for sparring. I had to realize that if my opponent is retreating, as much as I want to try and push their elbow and give them a pommel strike, that isn't the time. If they ran, I needed a new plan.

Of course, a decision tree can be quite complex if there are branches for every guard, movement, and parry, but I found even a simple and broad tree improved my responses.

After many mentally and physically exhausting lessons that illustrated these concepts, I developed an understanding of how to select and attack based on the situation, not just on what I *wanted* to do. I engineered a decision tree to help improve my sparring skills. I use the concept of a decision tree in all of my training now.

When I work on a new play in sparring, I examine the way it

would progress based off of variables. How would it fair against someone taller than I? Would an inexperienced opponent be likely to counter-attack and if so, can I predict where and how? What other attacks can I pair with the play? After considering a few basic "what-ifs," I select a couple of "ideal" situations to look for, so I know when to use a play. Once I engage, I then have my decision tree prepared in advance.

This has yielded more fruitful results than just trying to force a play to work when I'm in the ring. If my play fails, I try to take note of what my opponent was doing and how I can set up my attack better the next time, rather than just trying to perfect my power, form, and structure.

Drilling structure is necessary, but there is a lot more nuance to sparring. For me, structure and body mechanics were easier concepts to wrap my head around, compared to the chess-like calculations needed in sparring. Introducing the concept of a decision tree earlier can help mitigate a student's frustrations and misunderstandings.

JAY SIMPSON

BIG MAN'S FOLLY

"This Master with these swords signifies the seven blows of the sword. And the four animals signify four virtues, that is prudence, speed, strength, and boldness. Whoever wants to excel in this art will need to acquire these virtues."[98]

There is an axiom in many martial arts systems stating that technique can beat strength, without openly recognizing the naked advantage of size and strength of an opponent. It is implied to be an advantage, but is derided as a sort of brutish, unskilled quality that not everyone can possess due to the circumstances of a person's birth. In many cases it is demonstrated as being easily overcome by a system of technique. However, there are some cases where the gap in size and strength is simply too great to be overcome without weapons, and close combat weapons are a significant but imperfect equalizer. The use of these weapons still relies on the body of the user, and the larger opponent's greater ability to exploit strength, distance, and weight are still significant even with a sword in hand. What can a fencer do if they have this advantage, and what are the pitfalls of utilizing it?

I have learned about the big man's folly and how to use size and strength correctly over the years, because I am a big man. I'm 6'5" and weigh 280 pounds. I have overly relied on my size in the past. Why? It worked. For a while. Then, I gradually learned

---

98   *Fiore dei Liberi, Flower of Battle, Trans. Hatcher, 32.*

how best to *use* my size and not *rely* on my size.

"If you wish to grapple you should first assess whether your opponent is stronger or bigger than you, as well as whether he is much younger or older than you. You should also note whether he takes up any formal grappling guards. Make sure you consider these things first."[99]

The strengths of being larger as listed are obvious, especially if applied in sparring. A larger opponent can strike without being struck due to their greater reach. Their greater strength and leverage can force their opponents into unfavorable situations or even defeat their technique with direct force. Being larger in unarmed fighting is a nearly universally recognized advantage, in which most major competitive combats sports institute a system of weight classes. Larger fighters are recognized as having the ability to strike with greater force, at greater reach, and can apply greater weight and leverage in a grapple. So why is being larger not as advantageous when it comes to swordsmanship? One reason is the equalization of weaponry. No matter how large you are, everyone is still susceptible to the lethal effects of weapons to a nearly similar degree. It is also because the often-repeated axiom of "technique beats strength" is partially true, especially in the context of weapons and fencing.

"Note here that the squinter is a hew which breaks—in the hews and thrusts of the buffalo ([one] who acquires victory with power)"[100]

Many authors of historical texts recognize this omitted advantage of strength and size and speak about how to exploit it. The "buffalo" fighter is mentioned as an example of a larger, stronger fighter who only knows about his own strength and size and uses it in a direct and obvious manner. This ability to exploit strength arises from the larger fighter relying on their strength and size to such an extent that they do not recognize utilizing technique or even the danger of a smaller, more skilled opponent. The larger fighter can often fall into the trap of overestimating their natural ability to overcome all

---

99   *Ibid. 2.*

100   *Ringeck, A gloss on Liechtenauer's Zettel.*

obstacles, much in the way that their strength is derided as being unimportant next to technique. This results in the larger fighter having a narrow range of techniques and approaches, as they are most often able to force the situation into their favor. They become overconfident and careless as they have most probably won many fights by simply cowing their opponents, especially those with little practical experience in fighting. In short, being large can let you win and that can make you think it's the best way to win.

"You'll need to learn the guards of the Masters, how to distinguish the Students from the Players and the Players from the Masters, and finally the difference between the Remedy and the Counter."[101]

This seeming advantage is exploited in several ways. A smaller fighter can overcome the larger fighter's natural advantages with a greater understanding of distance, timing, technique, and most importantly, patience. The natural advantage of the larger fighter then becomes a detriment. Their movements become too committed and they waste too much time, their applied strength is used against them, and they are left frustrated, confused, and beaten or in a martial sense killed or maimed by a technique they did not see coming. This can lead to a complete collapse of their confidence in their ability and cause them to not use their natural advantages since they have clearly failed to consider a more skilled opponent.

> "If you want to learn the deeds of arms, my friend,
> See that you bear all that that this poem teaches.
> Be audacious in violence and young at heart.
> Have no fear in your mind, only then can you perform."[102]

A larger fighter's advantages also disappear when they are matched by a similar or even larger opponent. Suddenly, they find themselves on equal ground, or even in the small man's world. All their tricks of reach, size, strength, and force suddenly

---

101   *Fiore dei Liberi, Flower of Battle, Trans. Hatcher, 2.*
102   *Fiore dei Liberi, The Flower of Battle, Trans. Chidester.*

disappear. Attacks and techniques that they can typically suppress or break are made equal. Targets not typically taken against them are suddenly available. They find themselves in unfamiliar waters, trying not to sink. There is another often-repeated axiom, namely, "there is always a bigger fish in the sea." Larger fighters would do well to remember this in their training so they are not reminded of it under the pressure of competition or self-defense.

The larger fighter is best served by studying technique without forgetting to exploit their natural advantages when the situation arises. The larger fighter can learn the lessons of the smaller fighter and then use their natural advantages in a controlled and precise manner. Greater strength allied with precisely applied technique is extremely difficult to overcome, as it joins the two in a harmonious way. The natural yet ignorant confidence in size and strength is replaced with a technical confidence in the precise application of greater strength. It also compensates for the rare situations in which that advantage disappears but nullifies the skill gap and knowing how to use skill to defeat strength. Larger fighters should constantly be seeking to widen their ability outside of their natural advantages so that they are not relied on solely or even partly. When technique is coupled with strength you can live up to Fiore's words:

"You're all cowards and know little of this art. You're all just words without any deeds. I challenge you to come at me one after another, if you dare, and even if there are a hundred of you, I'll destroy all of you from this powerful guard."[103]

The final lesson to the big man's folly is to not be a bully and always use total and unrestrained force even when allied with technique. This can lead to the injury of relationships or can physically injure training partners. There are even times when this can happen accidentally even under ideal circumstances. The use of unrestrained strength and size due to lost temper or injured ego can get in the way of advancement in skill and the betterment of teachers, peers, and students. It can even cause direct and sometimes permanent injury unintentionally. Strength does

---

103   *Fiore dei Liberi, Flower of Battle, Trans. Hatcher, 20.*

not need to be proved, for it will be recognized and respected if used correctly. The key is to use strength appropriately in each circumstance to the greatest effect, including when not to use it. The lack of direct use of force from a larger opponent can be extremely confusing and a powerful tool to deceive opponents, in which case technique can be similarly applied in a way that would defeat a larger opponent.

Large fighters are at their best when they can judiciously apply their strength in both direct and unexpected ways. In this way their natural advantages are fully utilized, and they are not ignorant as to how their strength can be exploited by others. Still, no one is invincible and unbeatable no matter their advantages, and it should also be remembered that no physical attribute survives the ravages of time. Strength and speed only last so long and must be replaced with skill, knowledge, and deception for competition and instruction. This final big man's folly is that of growing old without being able to train and teach, but only how to compete, having lost his training partners to domination and bullying. Large fighters are well served to remember that they can be improved by all other fighters, big and small, and that they in turn can help to improve and teach all other fighters with their advantages and strength.

DANIA WRIGHT

TINY TROUBLES

What problems do tiny fencers face? Given that I am shorter than a montante (great sword) and weigh half as much as most people I fight, I can speak definitively on the subject. As an instructor with the Phoenix Society, I have met and taught (and fought) a huge variety of students of all shapes, sizes, and fitness levels. Needless to say, I've learned a few lessons along the way about teaching and doing HEMA for everyone.

First things first: The gear never fits, just accept it. I've never found a pair of jeans off the rack that fits, and HEMA gear is no different. While having the fanciest gear doesn't make you a better fighter, having badly fitting gear will absolutely make it harder for you or your students to drill and spar accurately, comfortably, and safely. Badly fitting gear can also lead to bad habits and bad fighting. Regardless whether you are short or tall, take extra care with off-the-rack gear and see about getting it custom sized, or at least shaping it to your frame.

Students who are struggling to translate a drill or slow play into sparring may be fighting gear without realizing it, especially with critical points like gloves and masks. A good example of this was with a student who struggled with lateral movement when sparring, despite displaying good footwork and measure during drills. Swapping an oversized back-of-the-head protector for a better fitting model allowed them to freely turn their head and regain a large amount of their peripheral vision, leading almost immediately to more confident footwork and sparring because they could actually see their surroundings!

Your mask is extra important, because when you're short everything comes at you from above. Hits to the head are the most common attacks smaller fencers face, partly because the head is a valuable target and partly because your head is where everybody else's chest is. This is both a problem and a benefit. Often taller fencers will misjudge where your head is; I have had powerful and well-structured cuts thrown at me and miss as they sail harmlessly over my head.

The taller fencer in this equation was acting out the next problem that arguably all fencers have on some level—adapting your plan and techniques for your own body and for each different opponent. There is no such thing as a perfectly average fencer; each of us has differences in body geometry, physicality, and experience that mean changing the way we fight. I am often asked if I can "do" the plays, or if I have to change them or do something different. The answer depends on the play and the opponent; given how much of HEMA is the art of interpretation, there is a remarkable amount of flexibility in how we apply different plays and techniques while remaining true to the text. As such, the first step is always to attempt the play as it is written in the source; after all, you have to know the rules before you bend them!

If the play doesn't work "out of the box," it's time to start investigating as to why. Trying to do a hip throw from Fiore dei Liberi's longsword manual, *Fior de Battaglia*, I discovered that a play that had worked perfectly on an opponent my size failed on a taller opponent. My arm was simply not long enough to reach the right spot on the other fighter's chest and neck to lever them over my hip. Rather than trying to use brute force to make the throw, I added a push to the chin that turned the opponent's head, breaking their structure and making the hip throw significantly easier. The trick then is to be able to read my opponent during sparring and quickly choose how to respond— the regular play, or the modified play? Do I push their elbow or do I push myself around their elbow? This is the challenge all fencers, short and tall alike, will face: in the heat of the moment, can you adapt to your opponent?

The best way to work on this is to practice on fighters of all shapes and sizes; if you are an instructor pay attention to the way your students respond to new fighters. Being short, tall, tiny, or anything else doesn't make you an inherently worse fencer, nor a better one. But it does mean taking extra time to figure out what works for you.

JACOB RUSSELL & REECE NELSON

Jacob Russelll

PHYSICAL LIMITATIONS

JACOB RUSSELL

M y great mistake was myself.
It wasn't my fault! I was hit by a truck in 2010. The damage was extensive. Both to the truck that struck me and to my legs. My right knee was destroyed, my bones smashed, my skin torn, and I was in such bad shape that I needed titanium rods put into my left leg all the way from the ankle to the hip. My right knee has staples and screws in it. I needed four surgeries over the years, and a lot of recovery time. It was six months before I could use my left leg and a full year before my right leg could support my weight, which, as I was bed-ridden, had increased. Even after I could walk, my weight increased and I had an overall fat, limping and weak body.

I came to the Phoenix Society in 2018 unkempt, with a brace on my leg, and yet with a desire to learn about swords. It was such a new and terrifying experience that I barely sparred at first. I would participate in some drills, but then sit down. However, I kept showing up despite the fear of undoing any progress made to better my legs. Every time I showed up I practiced a bit more, and each time I could fight a little longer and move a little better.

The old masters said practice was necessary. For me, that was doubly so. I needed to learn how to fence, but I also needed to re-learn how to use my broken body.

By 2020, that body wasn't so broken. I've lost weight and gained muscle. I have gained endurance. Where before I couldn't walk, I can now run. When I fence with the longsword, I enjoy grappling and wrestling, something I could never imagine doing after my accident. I've become good at cutting under the training of Phillip Martin, I've placed in tournaments, I have helped teach others, and when Richard Marsden had a student point out an error he was making in a technique—that was me! The club had taught me to fence and to read the sources!

Your "bad HEMA" might be yourself. It was for me. Practice, patience, and a willingness to grow slowly but steadily have allowed me to overcome my limitations. It is my hope that others who in some way struggle can learn from me and know that with patience, reading, practice, and diligence you will improve. Take it from a guy flattened by a truck!

REECE NELSON

I know where Jacob is coming from. My name is Reece Nelson and I also have a disability. I was told, "you can't do HEMA the proper way, so you shouldn't pursue it at all."

That sort of comment I've received all my life because I'm a left leg amputee and I'm proud to say I never listened to such things!

I was born 2 1/2 months premature, with a level four brain bleed and my left leg had to be amputated above the knee due to the umbilical cord cutting the circulation. I was in the ICU for months along with my twin brother, Adam. Sadly, he passed away shortly after birth and most thought I wasn't going to survive either.

I survived and made a full recovery, but having my left leg amputated above the knee since birth has created a whole new level of challenge. My type of amputation is very rare. Most amputees lose their leg below the knee or right above the knee, which allows for a better fitting prosthesis. Mine is known as a hip disarticulation, which means I don't have much use of my hip, which makes walking very difficult, let alone doing a martial art.

Reece Nelson

Throughout my life I've had to adapt and make things work for me and I took that same approach when working through HEMA. The masters never taught someone how to approach their teachings as an amputee, however; they did offer us a great amount of detail into what to do and how to do it. I spent a lot of time working through the fundamentals and doing my best to understand the body mechanics and making HEMA work, leg or no leg!

Overtime, I developed good posture, balance and structure. I tried to focus on the things I did well at and not get caught up on the things I struggled with. I admit, I would get discouraged because as a practitioner I wanted to do everything, but I knew I was physically limited. I needed to get stronger first off. So, I decided to put on a 75 pound harness and pursue Harnischfechten, the armored fighting arts. Here is where I put all of my training to the test! I would have to take multiple breaks from standing on one foot for so long. My leg would be so fatigued from the weight that it would be shaking after performing a few drills. I couldn't breathe, hear anything and my vision was limited, everything was telling me "you shouldn't do this" or " you should quit" or "this just won't work the way you are."

But, I stuck with it and I gradually became stronger. I discovered wearing harness actually benefited me wearing a prosthesis. Before I would slip out of the socket if I stepped too wide, now with the armored fauld it created a "wall" and prevented me from slipping out of the socket. I've found that my balance has improved since wearing full harness as well. All of these things have slowly helped me improve my daily life as an amputee. Like Jacob, I've worked through my disability and become stronger for it.

Since I've been doing HEMA I've received an overwhelming amount of support from the community. I've received messages expressing how people have found it inspiring to see someone doing this as an amputee, (in full harness no less) and others have reached out to me asking how to get involved in Harnischfechten from watching our YouTube channel "Pursuing the Knightly Arts".

And so, I want to echo Jacob with the idea that your "Bad HEMA" may have been out of your control, but through study, patience, dedication and determination you will see results. I know I did!

PHILLIP MARTIN

CUTTING

When teaching cutting classes at the Phoenix Society, one of the most common issues that I see with beginning cutters is that they attempt to perform cuts in the same way they have been taught to fence, before they have mastered the basics of cutting. Three prime examples of this issue that will be discussed here are first, cutting to the guard of long-point; second, circling the target while cutting; and third, holding back while cutting, since swinging with lethal intent is something that new fencers learn to avoid for the sake of safety.

In order to address the first issue, I explain to the student that intentionally cutting to long-point will invariably result in the sword decelerating while the blade is still inside the mat. This is a recipe for frustration. To perform a successful cut, the cutting motion must continue all the way *through* the target, not just *to* the target. When I observe short cuts occurring, I ask the student to back up, stand out of measure from the mat, and practice the descending cut through the air until they can perform it consistently through the entire arc of the cut. They must do this without trailing the tip of the sword behind the cut or slowing their cut down prematurely.

Issue number two, stepping to the side while cutting, is something that I occasionally see in both new and experienced cutters. When fencing, it is often a great idea to circle your opponent, moving offline to create an opening for a strike. But if, for example, a cut is being delivered from right to left while the cutter is circling the target toward their right, then the power of the cut is being robbed due to the fact that the cutter's body is moving in the opposite direction of their cut. To address this, I typically suggest that the cutter move toward the target, rather than around it. The forward motion will allow sufficient force to be generated for a successful cut.

The third issue results from the fact that cuts delivered while sparring are never intended to injure your opponent. A fencer never cuts to a point inside of their opponent or cuts through their arm or leg! Students usually practice avoiding overly powerful cuts that will injure their training partners. This can cause an issue with their cutting practice. One of the cuts where I most commonly see this issue manifest itself is in the rising cuts. Students will cut *to* the target, rather than *through* the target. To help the student overcome this issue, I typically recommend they imagine that they are cutting a target past the mat that they are actually cutting. I tell them to visualize cutting that imaginary target and ignore the actual mat. This is a helpful recalibration tool that will let them gain the feeling of successfully cutting through the target and help them to break this habit.

I believe that it is important for HEMA students to recognize that fencing and cutting practice often have competing goals, and therefore should be trained separately until the student is proficient at both. Training to properly fence will help the new cutting student avoid bad habits that can develop from cutting practice. Once the HEMA student has mastered the fundamentals of cutting, they can begin to apply what they have learned where and when it is appropriate. There is always a tradeoff between delivering a cut in the most powerful and effective way and fencing in a martially valid way that won't get you killed in a fight. It is important to understand that a martially sound cut from a fencing standpoint may not be optimally powerful. And that is okay! Understanding the underlying principles of how to cut well will allow you to deliver the most effective cut under the given fencing constraints.

Conclusion

The art of fencing is by its very nature contentious, and this is part of the reason why the masters were so opinionated. Fencing pits two people against one another in what may be a fatal encounter. Those who taught fencing were often selling a product (their teaching). They were selling themselves and their art as something you could rely on in a life-or-death struggle, and so it is no surprise that these masters of old ridiculed their rivals. For them, fencing was a financial and a life-or-death competition.

There were many reasons to point out bad fencing. First, it could get you killed. Second, by denigrating others a master tried to make himself look wise in a sea of fools. Third, a master by showing his superior methods made it clear that those who worked with him were going to have an edge in a martial encounter.

Looking at a collection of masters from the 1300s to the 1700s we can see that they did agree on some principals. There were (near) universally accepted habits that were seen as bad fencing. The fact that so many masters call out the same follies in others lets us know that the bad habits were commonly seen.

When learning HEMA today we must remember that the context of a martial art matters. Fiore dei Liberi's Flower of Battle was never meant to be taught to a great mass of people who would possibly end up facing one another. It was meant to be taught in secret so that Fiore's techniques could be used to defeat the common and bad fencing habits of others.

In the rapier treatises, whole sections are dedicated to how to fence against someone who doesn't know how to fence. A 17th century duelist may very well encounter more people with bad fencing habits than good ones; Giganti says as much, writing that most people you meet on the street have no idea how to use the sword at their side.

For those learning HEMA today, understanding bad practices is important and they should be utilized. If you are an instructor, you should learn the bad fencing habits and use them against your students. Why? So that the techniques the students are learning can actually work. If students only fight competent and skilled people, they will miss out on what their martial art was actually for which was fighting people who were dangerous, yes, but didn't fully know the art of fencing.

Consider this in a modern context. If you learn karate for self-defense then you should be prepared to fight an untrained thug with karate. Why? You are more likely to get into a self-defense situation with someone other than a black-belt. HEMA is no different and students should know how to fight the dangerous, timid, wild and reckless as well as competent fighters. The art is about fighting a wide variety of opponents! It should also be remembered that using bad HEMA can be an eye-opener for students. When I have a new student who is full of bad habits fence for the first time, they can sometimes end up striking or stabbing their experienced opponent. New fencers can be some of the most dangerous, a fact the masters of old mentioned. As one German proverb goes, "Even as an experienced swimmer can drown, so can an experienced fencer be defeated by a novice." So that your students don't metaphorically drown, it is good to fight them in a variety of ways including using the techniques the masters warn against!

While the masters were in general agreement on some bad habits, they were divided on others. This too can be useful for students and instructors of HEMA today. Fiore dei Liberi encourages waiting in a guard and counter-fighting. Many other masters explicitly warn against this. Does this mean Fiore is wrong? No. What it means is that you need to understand the weakness of his system. The masters often stated that those who wait in guard are either very good or very foolish. By waiting it becomes too hard to respond in time to a determined opponent. Critics say waiting in guard opens you up for deceits and feints. And so, if you are learning Fiore's art then you should learn to wait in a guard and prepare for an opponent who is dedicated or who will use feints. How do we know? Other masters tell us this in their criticism.

Conversely, those fencing against someone who is waiting in a guard can take from the wisdom of the past masters and try to pressure their opponent the way the masters of the past would. The masters' complaints about fencing informs us today as to what to expect and how to respond.

The masters say feints must be performed with skill or they're not worth doing. So learn to sell your feints and recognize poorly delivered ones in others.

The masters say cutting without a step leads to a weak blow. Recognize such disjointed attacks in others and intercept them with strength and practice on your own to strike with the step.

The masters say being timid and waiting in guard is a bad idea. So, if waiting in a guard be ready to transition to offense if the opportunity arises and prepare yourself for possible feints and strong attacks. If you see another waiting in a guard, use feints and direct attacks to get them to move the wrong way or move too slowly.

The masters say voids are pretty but are dangerous to perform. And so, learn how to perform them in a variety of settings and understand how to counter them.

The masters say parrying is not as good as single-time fencing. Learn to parry well and safely and learn to counter the parries of others!

The bad fencing the masters call out, even when they disagree on what bad fencing is, can be something you can learn from. Use it to know your own weaknesses and use it to capitalize on the common mistakes made by others.

In the modern setting we are discovering the bad habits of the past. Bad fencing in the 1300s carried over into the 1600s and is still with us today. However, we have new bad habits to look at about which the masters said little or nothing at all. Some masters warn about wearing ostentatious clothing that may tangle you up, but they spend very little time on "gear" as it were. Today, in our safe sparring culture, our gear is something that may lead to bad fencing habits. As Dania noted, one of her students had back-of-the-head protection that was too large and thus limited their movement. Jacob discussed how debilitating physical injury can be overcome. Phil noted how too much sparring can lead to failures in cutting, and he gave concrete examples of how to cut with power and the core, something the masters only mention obliquely. These are the problems of today that we must tackle alongside the historical issues of fencing.

Bad HEMA still exists. As we understand the sources more we will come upon new issues and problems to overcome. We must look to the past to help us in the present. We must overcome the problems of past fencers yet prepare ourselves to encounter them. Finally, we must look at our own training today and uncover what leads to poor fencing and how we can overcome it.

We must learn bad HEMA to develop good HEMA.

Acknowledgements

I would like to thank the researchers, translators and compilers of the sources. Their work on discovering, translating and presenting the written words of the historical masters is what allows HEMA to exist. If you enjoyed Bad HEMA be sure to go through the bibliography and purchase a book or visit a website. The HEMA community is a small one, so you can help by being a patron of their work.

Thanks to the Phoenix Society of Historical Swordsmanship and all of its members for participating and in some cases contributing to Bad HEMA.

Ben Blythe provided photography. Thank you for the numerous visits to get the shots we needed.

Jay Simpson for the cover and his contribution.

Special thanks to Jeff Kemper, my editor for his diligent work.

John Hackett for the photograph of Reece M. Nelson and Reece for his contribution.

Angel Uribe for the photograph of Phillip Martin.

And finally, thanks to Henry Snider who has done layouts for all of my books for years.

BIBLIOGRAPHY

Chidester, Michael (trans). "Fiore dei Liberi." Wiktenauer. Accessed 2020. https://wiktenauer.com/wiki/Fiore_de%27i_Liberi

Chidester Michael (trans). "Pol Hausbuch." Wiktenauer. Accessed 2020. https://www.wiktenauer.com/wiki/Pol_Hausbuch_(MS_3227a)

Forgeng, Jeffery L. *The Art of Combat: A German Martial Arts Treatise of 1570*. Barnsley: Frontline Books, 2015.

Forgeng, Jeffery L. Collectanea: *The Arms, Armour and Fighting Techniques of a Fifteenth-Century Soldier*. Woodbridge: The Boydell Press, 2018.

Hatcher, Colin. *The Flower of Battle: MS Ludwig XV13*. Phoenix: Tyrant Industries, 2017.

Kirby, Jared. Jeanette Acosta-Martinez and Ramon Martinez (trans). *Italian Rapier Combat: Capo Ferro's "Gran Simalcro."* Barnsley: Frontline Books, 2010.

Koepp, Cindy (trans). "Jeronimo Sanchez de Carranza." Wiktenauer. Accessed 2020. https://www.wiktenauer.com/wiki/Jer%C3%B3nimo_S%C3%A1nchez_de_Carranza

Leoni, Tom. *The Art of Italian Rapier, Salvator Fabris*. Chivalry Bookshelf, 2005.

Leoni, Tom. *The Complete Renaissance Swordsman: A Guide to the Use of All Manner of Weapons: Antonio Manciolino's Opera Nova (1531)*. Wheaton: Freelance Academy Press, 2012.

Leoni, Tom. *Venetian Rapier: Nicoletto Giganti's 1606 Rapier Fencing Curriculum*. Wheaton: Freelance Academy Press, 2010.

Mahon, Andrew (trans). "The Art of Fencing, or the Use of the Small Sword." Gutenberg Press. Accessed 2020. https://www.gutenberg.org/files/12135/12135-h/12135-h.htm

Marshall, Phil and Caroline Stewart and Piermarco Terminiello. *La Scherma: The Art of Fencing, Francesco Ferdinando Alfieri*. San Bernardino: Vulpes, 2017.

Musashi, Miyamoto. "The Book of the Five Rings." Holy Books. Accessed 2020. http://www.holybooks.com/wp-content/uploads/The-Book-of-Five-Rings-by-Musashi-Miyamoto.pdf

Pendragon, Joshua and Piermarco Terminiello. *The Lost Second Book of Nicoletto Giganti (1608)*. Leicestershire: Fox Spirit Books, 2013.

Reich, Steven and Piermarco Terminiello. *Treatise* on the *Subject of Fencing*. San Bernardino: Vulpes, 2017.

Silver, George. "Paradoxes of Defense." PBM. Accessed 2020. http://www.pbm.com/~lindahl/paradoxes.html

Swetnam, Joseph. "The Schoole of the Noble and Worth Science of Defence." 17th Century English Fencing. Accessed 2020. http://www.swetnam.org

Terminiello, Piermarco (trans). "Alfonso Falloppia." Accessed 2020. https://wiktenauer.com/wiki/Alfonso_Falloppia#Sword_Alone

Terminiello, Piermarco (trans). "Jacopo Monesi." Wiktenauer. Accessed 2020. https://www.wiktenauer.com/wiki/Jacopo_Monesi

Tobler, Christian (trans). "Fechtbuch Geschriebenn." Wiktenauer. Accessed 2020. https://wiktenauer.com/wiki/Johan_Liechtnawers_Fechtbuch_geschriebenn_(MS_Dresd.C.487)

Tobler, Christian (trans). "Johannes Liechtenauer." Wiktenauer. Accessed 2020. https://wiktenauer.com/wiki/Johannes_Liechtenauer#Treatise

Trosclair, Christian (trans). "Peter von Danzig." Wiktenauer. Accessed 2020. https://wiktenauer.com/wiki/Peter_von_Danzig_zum_Ingolstadt

Trosclair, Christian (trans). "Sigmund Rigneck." Wiktenauer. https://wiktenauer.com/wiki/Sigmund_ain_Ringeck#Long_Sword_Gloss

Windsor, Guy. *Veni Vidi Vici*. The School of European Swordsmanship. 2013.

BIBLIOGRAPHY

[Anonymous]. *Pol Hausbuch*. 1389-1494? Translated by Michael Chidester. In "Pol Hausbuch (MS 3227a)." Wiktenauer: A HEMA Alliance Project. Accessed 2020. https://www.wiktenauer.com/wiki/Pol_Hausbuch_(MS_3227a).

Alfieri, Francesco Ferdinando. *La Scherma: The Art of Fencing*. Translated and edited by Caroline Stewart, Phil Marshall, and Piermarco Terminiello. San Bernardino: Vulpes, 2017.

Capo Ferro, Ridolfo. *Italian Rapier Combat: Capo Ferro's 'Gran Simalcro'*. Edited and presented by Jared Kirby. Translated by Jeanette Acosta-Martinez and Ramon Martinez. Barnsley, UK: Frontline Books, 2010.

de Carranza, Jeronimo Sanchez. *The treatise of the Philosophy of Arms and of the true Skill and of the aggression and defense of Christianity*. Translated by Cindy Koepp. In "Jeronimo Sanchez de Carranza." Wiktenauer: A HEMA Alliance Project. Accessed 2020. https://www.wiktenauer.com/wiki/Jer%C3%B3nimo_S%C3%A1nchez_de_Carranza.

dei Liberi, Fiore. *The Flower of Battle*. Translated by Michael Chidester. In "Fiore dei Liberi." Wiktenauer: A HEMA Alliance Project. Accessed 2020. https://wiktenauer.com/wiki/Fiore_de%27i_Liberi.

dei Liberi, Fiore. *The Flower of Battle: MS Ludwig XV13*. Translated by Colin Hatcher. Phoenix: Tyrant Industries, 2017.

di Grassi, Giacomo. *True Art of Defense*. Translated by Norman White. Wiktenauer: A HEMA Alliance Project. Accessed 2020. https://wiktenauer.com/wiki/Giacomo_di_Grassi#The_True_Art_of_Defense.

Docciolini, Marco. *Treatise on the Subject of Fencing: Marco Docciolini's 1601 Fencing Treatise*. Translated by Piermarco Terminiello and Steven Reich. San Bernardino: Vulpes, 2017.

Fabris, Salvator. *Art of dueling: Salvator Fabris' Rapier Fencing Treatise of 1606*. Translated by Tommaso Leoni. Highland Village, TX: Chivalry Bookshelf, 2005.

Falloppia, Alfonso. *New and Brief Method of Fencing*. Translated by Piermarco Terminiello, Bergamo, Italy: Printed by Comin Ventura, 1584. "Alfonso Falloppia." Wiktenauer: A HEMA Alliance Project. Accessed 2020. https://wiktenauer.com/wiki/Alfonso_Falloppia#Sword_Alone.

Giganti, Nicoletto. *The 'Lost' Second Book of Nicoletto Giganti (1608)*: A Rapier Fencing Treatise. Translated by Joshua Pendragon and Piermarco Terminiello. Leicestershire: Fox Spirit Books, 2013.

L'Abbat, Monsieur. *The Art of Fencing, or the Use of the Small Sword*. Translated by Andrew Mahon. Project Gutenberg. Accessed 2020. https://www.gutenberg.org/files/12135/12135-h/12135-h.htm.

Liechtenauer, Johannes. *Johannes Liechtenauer's Written Fencing Book*. Translated by Christian Tobler. In "Johan Liechtnawers Fechtbuch geschriebenn (MS Dresd.C.487)." Wiktenauer: A HEMA Alliance Project. Accessed 2020. https://wiktenauer.com/wiki/Johan_Liechtnawers_Fechtbuch_geschriebenn_(MS_Dresd.C.487).

Liechtenauer, Johannes. *Die Zettel [A Recital on the Chivalric Art of Fencing]*. Translated by Christian Tobler. 1448? In Wiktenauer: A HEMA Alliance Project. Accessed 2020. https://wiktenauer.com/wiki/Johannes_Liechtenauer#Treatise.

Meyer, Joachim. The Art of Combat: A German Martial Arts Treatise of 1570. Translated by Jeffery L. Forgeng. Barnsley, UK: Frontline Books, 2015.

Monesi, Jacopo. Objections and Admonishments on the Subject of Fencing. Translated by Piermarco Terminiello. In "Jacopo Monesi." Wiktenauer: A HEMA Alliance Project. Accessed 2020. https://www.wiktenauer.com/wiki/Jacopo_Monesi.

Musashi, Miyamoto. The Book of the Five Rings. Holybooks.com. Accessed 2020. http://www.holybooks.com/wp-content/uploads/The-Book-of-Five-Rings-by-Musashi-Miyamoto.pdf.

Rigneck, Sigmund. A gloss on Johannes Lichtenauer's Die Zettel. Translated by Christian Trosclair. In "Sigmund Rigneck." Wiktenauer: A HEMA Alliance Project. https://wiktenauer.com/wiki/Sigmund_ain_Ringeck#Long_Sword_Gloss.

Silver, George. Paradoxes of Defense. London: Printed for Edward Blount 1599. Accessed 2020. http://www.pbm.com/~lindahl/paradoxes.html.

Swetnam, Joseph. The Schoole of the Noble and Worthy Science of Defence. London: Printed by Nicholas Okes, 1617. Swetnam.org: 17th Century English Fencing. Accessed 2020. http://www.swetnam.org.

Von Danzig, Peter. A gloss on Johannes Lichtenauer's Die Zettel. Translated by Christian Trosclair. In "Peter von Danzig zum Ingolstadt." Wiktenauer: A HEMA Alliance Project. Accessed 2020. https://wiktenauer.com/wiki/Peter_von_Danzig_zum_Ingolstadt.

ART

Courtesy Wiki-Commons / Creative Commons USA

A Duel of Palfries 18th century

Cape to Face, Heussler

After the Duel by Eugène Isabey

Liechtenauer

Albion Meyer's Munich Medieval Sword

German longsword fencing

Knights Dueling

Boar's Tooth, Fiore de Liberi, Flower of Battle, MS Ludwig XV13

Sword in One Hand, Fiore de Liberi, Flower of Battle, MS Ludwig XV13

Envelopment, Fiore de Liberi, Flower of Battle, MS Latin 11269

Condottieri, Lord Leighton

Medieval battle, 15th century

Longsword fencing, Meyer, MS A4

Cuts of the Sword, Phillipo Vadi, Codex 1324

Sword and Dagger, George Silver, Paradoxes of Defense

Rapier, Meyer, MS A4

Sword and Buckler, Di Grassi

Rapier and Cape, Salvator Fabris, Science of Arms

Rapier and Dagger, Salvator Fabris, Science of Arms

Rapier Pass, Salvator Fabris, Science of Arms

Rapier and Dagger, Capo Ferro, Great Representation of the Art of Fencing

Lunge, Capo Ferro, Great Representation of the Art of Fencing

Index

Richard Marsden has been fencing for decades and has been involved in Historical European Martial Arts since the early 2000s. He teaches history for a living. He is the author of several books including, Polish Saber and HEMA in its Historical Context, an interpretation of Fiore dei Liberi's treatise, and author of several science-fiction and fantasy works. He, along with John Patterson, run the Phoenix Society of Historical Swordsmanship. He is Master of Land Warfare courtesy AMU. His wife is incredibly tolerant of his eccentricities as are his three cats.

Printed in the USA
CPSIA information can be obtained
at www.ICGtesting.com
LVHW072250111124
796310LV00006B/111